THE RIP-OFF BOOK

VICTOR SANTORO

Loompanics Unlimited
Port Townsend, Washington

THE RIP OFF BOOK

Published by:
Loompanics Unlimited
PO Box 1197
Port Townsend, WA 98368

ISBN 0-915179-18-0
Library of Congress Catalog Card Number 84-81631

Contents

INTRODUCTION

The purpose of this book is to outline the basic principles of fraud and specific techniques fraud artists use to milk the public. The reader will learn to protect himself against many types of fraud by understanding the ways in which con men work. He'll also learn to protect his interests in transactions which fall into a gray area. These are transactions which, although not fraudulent in the eyes of the law, are yet shady and filled with danger for the innocent consumer.

We shall see that there is no clear dividing line between honest deals and frauds, and that there is an element of deception in many transactions.

The scope of this book will be limited, giving certain areas little or no attention. Gambling, for example, is a lucrative field for cheats, and most people should be aware that there is a risk of being defrauded when they gamble. It seems unnecessary to pound very hard upon this point.

Sophisticated white-collar crimes, such as embezzlement, bribery and kickbacks, will get no attention because victims are corporations, the officers of which are well-versed in the means of protection and detection. Employee thefts of various sorts, from physically stealing goods to faking expense account vouchers, affect ordinary citizens in that they can result in higher prices, but will not be covered because there is nothing the consumer can do about them.

The focus of this book will be on frauds aimed at working people and small businessmen, concentrating on the principles and techniques involved. The reader will learn how to forestall fraud by recognizing the methods and avoiding the traps. In this regard, there will be much discussion of borderline areas, not legally defined as fraud, and we shall see that there are many deceptive practices used without infringing the law because the law seems to be one step behind the clever fraud artist.

There will be outlines of methods by which the consumer can protect himself, both passively and actively. Finally, unlike most

1

consumer-oriented publications, this one contains explanations of the means of overt counter-attack against fraud artists, in an effort to help the reader understand that he or she does not have to be a passive and helpless victim because of the impotence of law-enforcement agencies.

A SHORT GLOSSARY OF TERMS

CON, CON MAN, CON GAME. This comes from the word "confidence," and originally was used in the sense that the fraud artist operated by gaining the victim's confidence.

MAIL DROP. An accommodation address which permits the fraud artist to receive mail at other than where he lives. While the Postal Service offers patrons mail boxes, it requires that the renter of a mail box provide his correct name and address. It is a crime to rent a post office box under an assummed name. Postal inspectors monitor closely the traffic to P.O. boxes and are alert to their use for fraud. Private operators, on the other hand, need observe no such restrictive regulations, and they rent their addresses to anyone who puts up the money. Their customers often have furtive purposes, but not necessarily criminal ones. Those seeking sexual contacts, for example, who write to "swinger's" clubs, often do not give their home addresses, either because they lead secret lives and do not want their families to know, or because they want to screen their mail without letting the writers know where they can be reached. Also known as "letter drop," "mail forwarding service," and "remailer."

MARK, JOHN, PATSY, PIGEON, SUCKER, are all synonyms for victims.

PENCIL. A front man in the operation of a dubious enterprise. The Pencil is often a legitimate accountant or lawyer, who does not know the real nature of the business. The Pencil is often used in the more elaborate fraud schemes, such as taking over and milking a legitimate business, not in what we call consumer fraud.

SHILL. A confederate or collaborator of the fraud artist. A shill will often pose as a customer at an "auction," bidding up the price and leading the suckers on. He will also serve as a third party in a gambling scheme, a "pigeon drop," or a "Murphy" game. Also known as a "Steerer."

WHAT IS FRAUD, ANYWAY?

In attempting to define "fraud," we'll gain an insight into why fraud artists are so hard to stop and prosecute. The same problems we have in defining it trouble legislators and police, and make arrest and prosecution very difficult.

Most of us know what we mean by fraud. We can say that fraud is an act to take money or other valuables from another person, for profit, and by means of deception. That's a simple definition, avoiding fancy words and legal terms.

Let's break down that definition and examine each part:

Taking money from another is often legal, when there is an honest transaction, such as working for it, or selling an honest product.

There's nothing wrong with making a profit, as everyone who works for a living faces the problem of selling his time or product for a profit. However, the question of how much profit is legal or legitimate is one that concerns lawmakers very much. Every several years, for example, the media present stories of defense contractors charging the Government extraordinarily high prices for simple items available at a supermarket or hardware store for a tiny fraction of the price. Selling a bolt or a pair of pliers for hundreds of dollars certainly appears illegitimate, although a prosecution for fraud is unlikely.

Deception is the key to fraud, and the hardest element to prove. Except in the case of a well-known or well-established fraud scheme, such as check kiting, it is very difficult to prove that there is intent to defraud.

Let's look at a few examples to see how hard it is to prove fraud exists:

Many people look for "investment" items they can buy in the expectation of either returns on their money, such as dividends, or being able to sell at a profit later on. When a seller offers a piece of real estate, and suggests that it will go up in price in years to come, it could be an honest transaction or it could be a fraud, depending on whether the seller knows the real estate is worthless and has no hope of appreciating. Proving what is in his mind is the hard part.

When a doctor advises a patient to have unneeded surgery or other treatment, he could be seeking to line his pockets, or he could be making an honest mistake. This, too, is very hard to prove, and very few doctors lose their licenses over this issue and almost none are prosecuted, although the amount of unnecessary surgery and treatment in this country is appallingly high.

In many cases, the seller is promoting something intangible, such as happiness. "Lonely hearts clubs," for example, are selling the prospect of a romantic relationship, and the situation is such that they cannot control whether or not two people so introduced will be able to establish a long-term relationship. This, too, makes prosecution very difficult.

When a seller offers goods or services and the buyer is disappointed, it might be fraud, or it might be an honest disagreement over the terms of the sale or the nature of the product or service. In many instances, it is a matter for civil litigation, not criminal prosecution.

For example, there are many fly-by-night home improvement rackets, but a contractor who sells a home improvement or repair that is defective is not necessarily a fraud artist. His firm may simply do sloppy work. In deciding whether or not to prosecute for fraud, the police must take into account the fact that the dividing line between fraud and legitimate business is so thin as to be invisible, and they will investigate to determine whether the accused is a long-established businessman who warranties his work and whether the majority of his customers are satisfied.

This theme will recur throughout this book. There are many businesses that operate on the thin edge of the law. Distinguishing between a legitimate one and a fraud operation is often impossible, partly because of inadequacies in the legal definition of fraud, and partly because frauds and legitimate enterprises resemble each other so closely, and often engage in the same tactics. In many instances, we must conclude that a business is not an outright, prosecutable fraud, but yet is "shady." Prominent examples of these are marriage counselors, sex clinics, weight loss and smoking clinics, and various "alternative health care" practitioners.

Unfortunately, the size and longevity of the business are not a reliable guide. In the examples cited above, of defense contractors overcharging the Government, the companies involved are among the largest in the country, and in the well-known electrical industries price-fixing case of the early 1960's, the names included such well-known companies as General Electric.

WHY FRAUDS?

To understand the problem, we have to look at what fraud is and what it is not. Fraud is a type of non-violent crime for profit. This simple-minded definition seems hardly worth putting on paper, but if we examine exactly what it means, we'll get a better understanding of what we're fighting.

The basic motivation for fraud is to make money. There are all sorts of ways of earning money, just as there are all sorts of crimes. The two fit together quite well. However, in this country crimes of violence carry severe penalties, and only the lowest, least-educated classes of criminals commit them. It seems easy to rob a bank, but that carries with it a Federal rap, and the FBI inevitably comes into the case. There is also the risk of a murder, which despite the rarity of the death penalty, is still a very serious charge.

The fact is that crimes against property have lesser penalties than crimes against the person. We value human life highly, and crimes that injure people are, under our laws, the most serious, whether they are for profit or not. Some crimes against the person have great emotional charges, and we can expect a judge to "throw the book" at a child molester more than a bad-check artist.

Prisons are full of violent criminals. There are several reasons for this:

■Violent criminals tend to be stupid, and more easily caught.

■Violent crimes attract more attention, tend to be more sensational, and get higher priority from the police.

■Generally, there are longer prison terms for violent crimes, and those convicted spend more of their lives in prison.

■There is more sympathy for the victim of a violent crime, and judges tend to hand down stiffer sentences.

■With prison overcrowding, parole boards are often enacting early release programs for convicts. They tend to release those who in their view pose the least danger to society. Nonviolent criminals tend to get earlier paroles.

■Perhaps most importantly, many frauds are not even in

violation of an enforcable statute, which makes conviction much harder.

MYTHS ABOUT FRAUDS AND VICTIMS

There are several myths about frauds, and the characteristics of victims, which have been floating around for years. These myths came about from a superficial understanding of how fraud artists work, and from ignorance of the varied methods they use. Let's take these apart one by one:

You can't cheat an honest man. *False.* You can cheat an honest man, if your scam is properly targeted. This myth is based on the naive idea that the only people vulnerable to fraud are those who are greedy, and who expect to get something for nothing, laying themselves open to the false promises of the fraud artist.

In fact, even people with the highest morals and the most modest ambitions are open to fraud. A good example is the "bank examiner swindle,"[1] in which a person claiming to be a bank examiner asks the victim, who has an account at the bank, to withdraw a large sum of money to help the examiner check up on the honesty of a teller who is under suspicion. The victim does not expect personal gain, but is simply seeking to aid the examiner in enforcing the law.

Another scheme which involves victimization of people who are not seeking great riches is the "Social Security" or "Welfare" investigator scheme, in which a person claiming to be an investigator for one of these agencies arrives at the home of someone who is retired, or on welfare, presents phoney credentials, and claims to be collecting overpayments.[2] The "investigator" demands that the victim hand over to him or her the amount of the overpayment.

Frauds all involve get rich quick schemes. This is a corollary to the first myth, and it too, is false. While it is true that a person who shows raw, naked greed lays himself open to this sort of deception, there are also many victims defrauded because of need, not greed.

The fake employment-service swindle, in which a job seeker pays the fraud operator a fee to cover the cost of a "background investigation,"[3] is a clear example of defrauding the needy. Another is the classic security-bond swindle, in which respondents to an ad offering a cashier's or teller's job are asked to put up a large sum of money as a security bond because the purported position involves handling large sums of money and the "employer" wants tangible evidence of good faith.[4]

The victim of a fraud is somewhat stupid. Again, not necessarily. Our Twentieth-Century society is so complicated that it is literally impossible for any one person to be knowledgable about everything he faces in daily life. Many successful operators exploit this, and offer products or services that pertain to the latest **developments in technology, or trendy fields. In the early 1960's** fast operators were selling nuclear bomb shelters. More recently there has been a rash of solar energy device sellers cashing in on one of the latest trends. "Survival" foods and supplies are another instance in which attaching a trendy label to ordinary merchandise enables an operator to hike the price to several times what other outlets charge for the same items.

From this we see that it is possible to defraud even knowledgable and sophisticated people because there are inevitably some areas in which even the cleverest person lacks the technical knowledge to evaluate the worth of a product or service. Another point is that, in many fields such as the stock market, the rules are so complicated that only an expert can understand them and those outside the field are at the mercy of the specialists.

Frauds involve only shady, fly-by-night operators. It is not true that frauds are perpetrated only by sleazy types who have no fixed address or established reputation. A recurring theme in this study of fraud is that the fraud artists operate on the borderline of legitimate business, and that in many cases there are legitimate businesses that operate in a fraudulent manner. We shall see, in examining the medical profession, employment and literary agencies, and other established businesses, that they often engage in practices which are technically legal, but have a foundation of deception.

An equally important point is that fraud operators often assume the trappings of long-established and legitimate concerns. An operator will set up a front that uses a name very much like that of a well-known company, and may even establish a well-appointed office which he claims is a branch of a real corporation.

NOTES

1. *Short Cons,* Scot Tinker, 1977, Eden Press, P.O. Box 8410, Fountain Valley, CA 92708, p. 7.

2. Ibid., p. 8.

3. *Crooks, Con Men, and Cheats,* Eugene Villiod, 1980, Gambler's Book Club Press, Box 4115, Las Vegas, Nevada 89106, p. 57.

4. Ibid., p. 58.

CRIME PAYS

This is an undisputed fact. Despite there being more people in prison today than ever before, crime still pays. However, we have to be careful to observe the limits, because not all crime pays. A jealous husband who murders his wife or lover is not doing it for profit, and gains only a temporary satisfaction, which he may later decide wasn't worth it.

To be precise, we should say that "crime for profit pays." Within this definition, there are all sorts of crimes for profit. Mugging and armed robbery are crimes for profit, but in relation to the risks of apprehension and the harsh penalties, they do not pay very well.

The gain from violent crimes is uncertain in most instances. "Great train robberies," in which the perpetrators get away with enough to retire for life, are very few. Mostly, violent crimes for profit are grubby gas station stickups in which the gain is a few hundred dollars at most, or muggings in which the gain may be only one or two dollars.

The risks are severe. An armed robber may be shot dead by the shopkeeper or by the police. Upon arrest, an armed robber is less likely to get bail than a non-violent criminal. Prosecution is easier, as there are few gray areas in violent crime. Sentences are longer. The prospect of parole or pardon is dimmer.

The smartest criminals are those who live by their wits. For them, crime really pays.[1] In many instances, the main reason is that many non-violent crimes are difficult to trace and prove. In fact, many are not even covered by the criminal code, but fall under the civil code.

A look at a few examples will illustrate the range of non-violent crimes and the difficulty of prosecution:

You are a storekeeper who accepts a bad check. The man who gave it to you had the required I.D., but it was false. You deal with many customers daily, and can give the police only an uncertain description, which makes the chances of his apprehension poor. Writing a bad check is a felony, but it is hard to enforce in practice.

You're shopping for a used car. The salesman tells you that the car you're scrutinizing is in good shape and well-maintained. It looks good to you, and is clean. You buy it, and find out later that it needs extensive repairs. The bill of sale states clearly that there is only a thirty-day warranty on the car, and the thirty days are up. You feel that the salesman misled you, and you're also kicking yourself for not having the car checked out by a mechanic before buying it. You have no recourse and have to eat your mistake.

You take out an insurance policy on your property. You suffer a loss and find that the insurance company will not pay you to replace it, although you insured it for your cost. The contract says, in the fine print, that the property is covered only for its depreciated value, while you have been paying premiums on its full value. The law stands on the insurance company's side, but you feel cheated because during the long discussion you had with the insurance salesman, he did not explain this to you.

You get an invitation to attend a showing of real estate tracts. The offer includes a dinner on the company, and you decide to attend, calculating that you'll at least get a free meal. You arrive at the office, and you and the other "guests" see a film depicting the property, which is several hundred miles from where you live and which you have never seen in real life. There are artist's renditions of a projected golf course, shopping center, and other improvements, and the salesman tells you that this property will be a good retirement site or investment for you. In front of you on the table is a pile of papers, which you start to read. The papers include sales brochures and a legal document. When you start to pick up the legal document, the salesman slams his hand down on it and continues to talk about the virtues of the property, making the offer seem so attractive that you sign a contract for it before you leave.

On your way out, you pick up the pile of papers. Upon reaching home, you look at the legal document, which is a statement by the state's real estate commission. This paper tells you that, regardless of anything the seller may have told you, you are purchasing the property at your own risk, and that there is no warranty that you are not purchasing a piece of swampland or a mountain peak, that the property may or may not have utilities, and that you should physically inspect it before signing any contract. Slowly, you get the feeling that you've been had. You consult your lawyer, who tells you that you should not have signed anything before you knew exactly what you were buying. You're now committed to make the time payments.

A water-softener salesman comes to your door. He gives you a plastic bucket of "free samples" in return for your agreeing to listen to him for a half-hour. He shows you the effect of hard water on plumbing, etc., and convinces you that the unit he sells is the best on the market, saying that it has a lifetime warranty. You sign a purchase contract, and a few days later the unit arrives at your house, with a crew to install it. A month later, the unit breaks down. You find that to get it repaired, you have to dismantle it and ship it several hundred miles. There is no repair facility in town. Upon further checking, you find that a local outlet sells a similar unit for half the price, and that this company has its own service department, which makes house calls.

A salesman shows up at your door, claiming he is doing a market survey. He tells you he will give you a stack of records if you'll answer a few simple questions. You let him in, and he tells you that he is looking for new customers, and that if you give him the names and addresses of several of your friends, he'll give you a substantial discount on a stereo for yourself. You agree, and get out your checkbook. He brings in a stack of records and a stereo set in a cabinet. After he leaves, you look closely at the records and find they are "cheapies" by obscure artists, on unknown labels. Some days later, a friend who is familiar with sound systems tells you that the set you purchased is of inferior quality and that you overpaid for it. You never hear from the salesman again, although you find out a friend to whom you led him bought one of his sets. Some days later, your stereo fails. When you try to telephone the company whom the salesman represents, you find the number has been disconnected.

You answer an ad relating to an investment opportunity. A salesman calls on you, telling you that you have a chance to invest in a company that will manufacture a new type of carburetor that doubles the gas mileage of any car. He shows you several brochures, and you think it is a good idea. You give him a check, he hands you a receipt, and you never hear from him again.

You answer an employment ad, feeling it is legitimate because the name of the company is familiar. When you arrive at the office, the "manager" tells you that you must invest some money to buy a stockpile of merchandise, and go on from there to build your own network of dealers. You sink a thousand dollars into this, and then find that persuading other people to buy the merchandise from you is far more difficult than you'd anticipated or been led to believe. Your lawyer tells you that you signed a contract that you would act as an independent dealer, that the parent company is not responsible for your success. You are left holding the bag.

Note that none of these schemes are ridiculous, something-for-nothing frauds. None of them involve anything outlandish, such as a machine for turning dirt into gold. None of them appear to involve any risk for the customer. None of them are even get-rich-quick schemes which promise huge profits instantly. They are all believable, which is why many people get taken in each year.

NOTES

1. *Crime Pays,* Thomas Plate, Simon and Schuster, New York, 1975.

WHY ARE WE VULNERABLE?

It seems shameful to admit we are vulnerable to fraud. It implies we are not very bright, that we can be outwitted. That is a degrading picture to paint of ourselves, yet to an extent, it is true.

It is a cliche that some of the sharpest minds in the country are working full-time to separate us from our money. Many of these people are not working at what most would call criminal pursuits. Those who work for advertising agencies, for example, are quite legally employed, even though their work is mainly devising new and more creative ways of telling lies.

Most of us have met people who seem to be natural-born schemers, whose minds are always working on ways to take advantage of someone else. Often, these people have very likable personalities, and inspire confidence, until we get to know them better. Most of us don't think along those lines, and thus are not prepared to resist a fraud.

Most of us do not seek to scheme, and do not even form the habit of thinking defensively. To most of us, transactions are straightforward affairs, in which we exchange a known quantity of money for a known product or service. Most of the time, we are not disappointed.

Another truism is that the world is a complex place, and life is getting more complicated every day. In daily life, we have to depend a lot on faith and trust. We assume without checking thoroughly that something we buy will be what we want. In buying a car, for example, we trust that it will get us from one place to another without breaking down, even though most of us are neither automotive engineers nor mechanics.

This is true of almost anything we buy. We cannot be specialists in everything, and cannot evaluate the quality of the many manufactured products we use each day. When we buy services, we are on even more slippery ground, as often we cannot evaluate whether or not we got our money's worth until after it is all over, and the best guide we have is experience with a certain provider.

Automobile mechanics are very variable in quality, and good advice is to stick with a mechanic we've found to be competent. Medical care is another, and much more serious, problem. Finding a good doctor can be very difficult, and since medical care is such a complicated subject, it is hard for a layman to discern whether or not a treatment or drug a doctor advises is either necessary or effective.

This brief review of the problems we face in normal transactions provides a good background to the difficulties in preventing our falling victim to fraud. In our complex Twentieth-Century industrialized society, we are accustomed to accepting products and services from people we hardly know, or don't know at all. In some cases, we buy sight unseen, as from mail-order catalogs, secure in the knowledge that **most mail-order operators** are honest. In other cases, we buy intangibles, such as insurance, and we depend on the reputation of the insurance company.

Most transactions are not as straightforward as we'd like them to be, but we can't help that. It is easy to detect, in a supermarket, whether a container of milk is sour or if fruit is spoiled. It is much harder to decide if a manufactured product will give us good service. That is why we tend to rely on third parties, such as the publications of various consumer groups and the standards set by the government or industry associations.

The pace of life is faster. We are being constantly pressured to make snap decisions in our buying. Merchandisers often do not allow us the time to make a deliberate judgement, as they present "limited offers" and "one-day sales." We have become accustomed to deciding on the spot.

Most of us have the sense to know that a big purchase requires more thought than a small one, that buying a car is a greater commitment than buying a pocket radio, because we have much more to lose if we make a bad decision, but even in this we often find almost irresistable pressure to *buy now!* Car salesmen, whether working for new car dealers or used-car lots, have well-developed sales skills and high-pressure tactics to push us into signing immediately, even when they are selling a perfectly legitimate car in good condition.

As previously mentioned, the dividing line between legitimate business and fraud is so thin as to be invisible. The similarity in tactics between fraud artists and legitimate businessmen blurs the distinction further.

Now that we've surveyed the social factors that make us vulnerable to fraud, let's tackle the hard part, our personal traits. A former manager for the Fuller Brush Company said that "Door-to-door selling is the post-graduate course in practical psychology."[1] This is true of both the legitimate salesman and the fraud artist. The fraud specialist is expert at taking advantage of our weaknesses. He knows how to "read" a person and assess vulnerabilities. This is not a magical skill and is not perfect. One of the best-kept secrets of salesmen is how often they fail to make a sale. This is also true of con men. Most of us will resist a con game most of the time. The basic principle of strategy, both in selling and in fraud, is not to waste time on those who are unlikely to buy, and move on quickly to someone who is more vulnerable.

Both salesmen and con men know that all of us have certain characteristics which may make us vulnerable. This is what they look for, and what they exploit:

Mind-set. This is a preconceived attitude that sometimes leads us to false conclusions. Right now, with the controversy over energy sources, many people have a mind-set that solar energy is safe, non-polluting, and economical. This opens the door to many fly-by-night types who sell cheap and ineffective solar energy devices. Many people are also prepared to accept various types of energy-saving devices uncritically, enabling salesmen and con men to sell them cheap timers at high prices in the belief they will save on fuel bills.

Stereotyping. This is a combination of social and personal attitudes that makes us more ready to accept certain types of people and presentations. We see certain people as "respectable" and others as disreputable. We tend to have more confidence in a person who is neat and dresses well, drives an expensive car and has a well-furnished office than we do someone who appears "hungry." We also tend to listen with more respect to someone who is articulate and well-spoken than to someone who has a poor vocabulary and uses bad grammar.

Allied with this are ethnic stereotypes. We are more likely to react positively to a person who is Caucasian, has an "American" sounding name, and speaks without an accent. This is changing, however, as each new generation grows up bringing with it new values.

Bargain-hunting. While most of us are sophisticated enough to know that we rarely, if ever, get something for nothing in the real world, and people do not give fortunes away, we still seek good deals. We know, for example, that it is possible for someone to buy stock in a company when the price is low and to make a profit by selling when the price goes up. We also know that prices in our "free-market" society are volatile and it is possible to get good deals by buying in the right place and the right time. Con men offer us spurious "good deals."

Suggestibility. Some people are prone to believe almost anything anyone tells them. Both salesmen and con men try to enhance suggestibility by appearing "respectable." Suggestibility warps judgement, and those who are very suggestible will often accept on "say-so" what the rest of us would not without further proof. A salesman or con man can tell a suggestible person by some physical signs. For example, someone who constantly nods "yes" while the pitchman is talking is showing suggestibility. Salesmen and con men also look for a gleam in the eye, a brightening of the expression, upon hearing of the "good deal."

Suggestibility can also be gauged by the person's willingness to accept the approach. Salesmen and con men never ring a doorbell and say they're there to sell a vacuum cleaner or uranium stocks. Instead, they tell a lie, claiming that they are conducting a survey, doing market research, or giving out gifts. Most of us know that when a stranger phones or rings the doorbell, he's not there to do us favors, but some accept this spurious explanation at face value. This gives the experienced salesman or con man an important indicator of his victim's suggestibility.

Laziness. Some of us are not especially suggestible, but are mentally lazy, and unwilling to do our homework in checking out claims. We do not bother to ask the right questions when we're confronted by a "deal," and do not bother to investigate further than reading the sales brochure. Although it is usually possible to check with the Better Business Bureau, references, or the police, victims of frauds don't do this.

Possibly the most important reason we're vulnerable is that *fraud artists are pros and we're not.* An amateur is at a distinct disadvantage when up against a pro. We can't hope to prevail against a professional boxer, despite some experience while in school. Although most of us have driver's licenses, we cannot hope to match the skill of a professional race driver. In the same way, we can expect to fail when up against a professional con man, unless we have ways of compensating for our deficiencies.

NOTES

1. Personal statement to the author.

PORTRAIT OF THE FRAUD ARTIST

The stereotypical image of the criminal is a dull, brutish lout more at home with a gun or blackjack than with a good book. This is utterly untrue of fraud artists. Let's look at the real fraud artists and see why they are so successful.

The term "con man" is accurate. Fraud artists are skilled at building confidence in the victim. "Con man" is inaccurate in one respect. The fraud artist may be either male or female. It's a mistake to think that fraud artists are all fast-talking, shifty-eyed sleazebags — on the contrary, they work very hard at looking respectable.

They tend to be very intelligent people. A common misconception, reinforced by those who preach that "crime does not pay," is that criminals are stupid, that they are low-life misfits who, if they had normal intelligence, would earn their livings honestly. In fact, fraud artists are among the elite of crime. It is mainly the stupid and untalented criminals who get caught and prosecuted successfully. The prisons are filled with failures in this field.

While it's true that street criminals tend to be young men who often straighten out after they mature completely, the picture is quite different in the realm of fraud. Fraud artists tend to be dedicated professionals, true career criminals who, if they are imprisoned, return to their preferred method of livelihood.[1] Fraud artists tend to be winsome, attractive people. They certainly are "street-wise," a skill which is of utmost value in conning the victim as well as conning the parole board in the unlikely eventuality of conviction and imprisonment.

They are good actors. Although probably unable to play serious roles upon the stage, their performances are tailored to the roles which they play in real life. This puts the victim at a disadvantage, as he is up against a "pro."

Perhaps most importantly, their performances and tactics are well-rehearsed. They work hard at perfecting their skills. They can put across a complicated deception without the guilt and unease the rest of us feel when telling lies.

NOTES

1. *Fraud Investigation,* Glick and Newsome, Charles C. Thomas, 1974, 2600 S. First St., Springfield, Illinois 62704, p. 8.

ANATOMY OF A FRAUD

We can dissect the operations of a fraud artist into component parts, in order to understand not only the basic deception but the dynamics of the process. Fraud is a transaction, an interaction, between two parties, and its success depends on some subtle and often intangible factors.

INCENTIVE

This is the first component. The victim must have an incentive to place himself in the hands of a fraud artist. In the classic swindles, the con man makes the initial approach, offering his get-rich-quick scheme. This is not always so, however. Some victims are lured by impersonal approaches, such as advertisements and word-of-mouth. It might seem strange that one fraud victim might give a recommendation to the fraud artist, but some fraud schemes are partly based on this, as we shall see. In other instances, a fortune-teller or faith healer may give the victim great satisfaction, and win a convert.

The incentive is usually some sort of benefit for the victim. It's a mistake to think this is always a tangible profit. Sometimes the motive is health and well-being, sometimes the good feeling that comes from helping others, as when making a gift to charity.

THE COME-ON

This is reinforcing the incentive. The con man establishes confidence in the victim, sometimes by presenting credentials, in other instances by sheer force of personality and salesmanship. The skills involved are exactly the same that salesmen and other more or less legitimate people develop.

THE SHILL

This is a third person, sometimes unwitting, but more often part of the scheme. A shill acts as a disinterested party, reinforcing the victim's participation. He can be a fake buyer at an auction, serving to bid up prices. He can be a supposedly unrelated third party in a pigeon drop. He can be a contributor in a "flop" scheme, etc., as we shall see.

THE SWITCH

This is the substitution of a fake for the article of value, which forms a part of many schemes. Sometimes the switch is as crude as substituting a lead brick for a gold brick. In other cases, there is no physical switch involved, but an intangible one, as in bait-and-switch advertisements.

PRESSURE

The con man often uses some form of pressure, to hurry the victim along and impede him from carefully considering the transaction. He often imposes a time limit, either by stating that the deal is a now-or-never offer, or by claiming that there is another buyer waiting, possibly with a better offer. This is why those who engage in con games are sometimes known as "hustlers."

THE BLOCK

This tactic is aimed at stopping the victim from reporting the incident to the police, and is often a carefully-planned part of the scheme. The victim might buy an item which he thinks has been smuggled, for example, in which case reporting to the police would involve a confession of wrong-doing. In other instances, the activity, while perhaps not outrightly illegal, is shameful. Schemes involving sex play upon this.

In yet other instances, the victim supplies his own block. Many instances of fraud go unreported because the victims are ashamed to confess that they have been outwitted. If the sum involved is small, the victim may decide he'll just write it off to experience.

Some schemes use anticipation of further reward as a block. In referral and commission schemes, the con man, by promising, and sometimes paying, commissions for prospects referred by the victim, turns him into an unwitting *steerer*, or *shill.*

Some victims never complain because they never realize they've been defrauded. A victim who buys a fake diamond, for example, may never have it appraised, and never find out it is bogus.

The block need not be permanent for it to succeed. For the con man's purpose, it need only keep the victim quiet for a limited time, enough for the con man to get out of town or to work his scheme on other victims.

Con games, although they vary greatly in style and substance, are all simply permutations of these basic elements. Con men are constantly thinking up new games, or new variants of the old ones.

ONE STEP AHEAD OF THE LAW

It's a fact that non-violent crime is more profitable than violent crime. It's also a fact that it is harder for the criminal justice system to cope with non-violent crime, and there are both fewer convictions and lighter penalities. In the case of fraud, judges and juries have a prejudice against the victim, seeing him or her as a victim of their own stupidity as well as of the criminal's scheme.

Fraud is an intellectual crime, not a physical one. It takes more brains to plan and carry out a fraud scheme than it does to execute a mugging. Except for the higher level of intelligence required, the mentality of the criminal is the same. He or she sees other people as prey, to be harvested for profit.

One important part of the problem is that the law often seems to be a step behind in coping with frauds. Violent crime is clear-cut and easily identifiable. Fraud often is not. This is the crucial point which makes apprehension and prosecution more difficult.

The criminal justice system is reactive. There must first be a crime: only then can the system act. Thinking about commiting a crime is not an indictable offense. Planning is, but proving conspiracy is very, very difficult.

A major component of the fraud artist's planning is in thinking up a scheme that will be difficult or impossible to prosecute. While there are laws on the books regarding fraud, the schemers are constantly thinking up new plans, and given the slow pace of the law enforcement authorities and the legislators, the laws covering frauds are usually one or more steps behind the acts.

Computer crime is an excellent example. There have been many, some of which remain undetected. There are few laws on the books covering computer crime, despite the warnings given by computer security experts. There is the typical lag between the discovery of a new type of crime and the implementation of a law to cover it.

The key to fraud is there is a willing victim. There is no coercion involved. For a criminal prosecution, it is necessary to prove intent to defraud, and sometimes the fraud operator can claim that the affair is simply a disagreement over the terms of a contract, which makes it a civil, rather than a criminal matter.

Just as the dividing line between legitimate business and fraud is very thin, the line between fraud and deception is also almost invisible. A fraud artist who tries to peddle a machine that changes one-dollar bills into twenties can definitely be indicted for fraud, but a company whose advertisements promise us that if we buy its product we will be happy cannot. Yet, there is deception in each instance.

One major reason for the slowness of the criminal justice system in responding to fraud is that in this country, the legislators are business-oriented. They are very reluctant to pass any law that may affect legitimate business, and only the most flagrant abuses will move them to act.

One example is the "Truth In Advertising Act." The shades of deception, and outright lies, promoted by advertisers finally became so notable that the United States Congress, after decades of neglect, passed a law.

Another example is the "Truth In Lending Law." Banks and finance companies had for generations concealed the true rates of interest from their customers until it finally became necessary to make it mandatory to disclose what the consumer would actually pay for the credit.

Only recently have there been laws that spell out precisely that certain previously common practices, such as turning back the odometer of a used car, are fraudulent and illegal. The reluctance and slowness of the government in reacting to fraud is one of the things which open the door to the creative fraud artist.

This background shows us the task of the fraud operator who succeeds: He finds a scheme that will earn him money, but which is not easily indictable because there is no law spelling out that what he's doing is illegal, although his intent is to deceive. The fraud operator who gets rich and stays out of prison is truly one step ahead of the law.

CLASSIC SWINDLES

Let's start our study of frauds by examining the classic swindles, the "oldies but goodies." These scams are very old, yet we find them still in use today, sometimes in their original versions, and sometimes with modification to bring them up to date.

Inevitably, the question comes up: "Why do these old scams still work?" The schemes are old, but the operators use them on new people, as each generation has to learn for itself the problems and mistakes that plagued its ancestors. P.T. Barnum allegedly said of suckers: "There's one born every minute," and he was right.

THE SPANISH PRISONER

This is the oldest known swindle, allegedly dating from 1588. The swindler approaches his mark with a letter, supposedly written by a person unjustly imprisoned in a Spanish castle. The letter states that a certain amount of money, which will serve to bribe his jailers, will secure his release. The letter also alleges that the prisoner has a treasure chest full of valuables, which he will share with the person who puts up the money for his freedom. The victim hands over the money to the swindler, who disappears.

It might seem incredible that anyone would fall for this today, but there are modern versions, as swindlers keep up with the times.[1] One is that the prisoner is incarcerated behind the Iron Curtain, or in a "Third World" country. The money requested may be for bribes, or to hire a force of mercenaries to mount a commando-style raid to rescue the prisoner. The treasure chest story is old, and the modern version is that the prisoner has a cache of bearer bonds, or a numbered account in a Swiss bank. The swindler tailors his story to the needs and fashions of the moment, which enables him to get more mileage out of an old con game.

THE PIGEON DROP

This one is only perhaps 200 years old, according to one source.[2] The victim "accidently" runs into the con artist on the street and they strike up a conversation. They soon find, as they are walking along, a wallet or pocketbook, or even a paper bag with a large sum of money inside. There is no identification in the wallet, and it seems they can keep the money with clear consciences. The con artist suggests that, to be on safe ground, he consult his lawyer to find out exactly how the law regards found money.

The con artist returns from the lawyer's office, saying the lawyer informed him or her the two finders are legally entitled to the money if nobody claims it, but that each must put up a "good faith" bond to establish their honest intentions and prove that they can return the money if it is claimed by the person who lost it. The victim withdraws a certain sum of money from the bank, hands it to the con artist, who claims that he'll deliver it to the lawyer to be put into an escrow account, and the victim never sees the con artist or the money again.

There are many variations possible in this swindle. The con artist may ask the victim to accompany him to the lawyer's office so they may both hear what the lawyer has to say. The lawyer takes charge of the money, and the victim returns with the "good faith" bond and places it in the lawyer's hands. The lawyer says if the money is unclaimed after six months, the finders can split it. This tactic enables the con artist and the "lawyer," who is his confederate and not really a lawyer, to work the scheme many times from the same rented office while their first victims are waiting out the six months. When the first victim returns to the "lawyer's" office, he or she finds the occupant has moved and left no forwarding address.

Another variant is the con artist asks for a bond from the victim, meanwhile giving the victim the package of money to keep in his safe deposit box. This deception involves the use of a "Michigan roll" or "gambler's roll," which is a roll of paper cut to the proper size with a few genuine bills on the outside. The original "find" may be real money, and in fact has to be if the swindler switches wallets, or packages, leaving the victim with the fake roll. They both go to the victim's bank, and the victim puts the fake package in his safe deposit box. He then withdraws the amount for the "bond" from his account, feeling safe because the amount of the "bond" is less than the amount supposedly in the package. The swindler then disappears.

THE ENVELOPE SWITCH

This old game usually requires a con artist and a confederate. A likely spot for the initial meeting is a bar, in which the artist strikes up a conversation with the mark. The con man claims to be a seaman, traveling salesman, or otherwise a stranger in town. He mentions that he wants to have a good time on his first night in town, and says he intends to go to a certain locale or to a house of prostitution. At this critical juncture, the confederate, who has been sitting nearby, comes into the conversation and tells the con man that he runs the risk of being robbed or "rolled" if he ventures into that part of town.[3] He suggests he leave the bulk of his money with the mark for safekeeping. The con man agrees, but suggests that the mark take the money and place it in an envelope, adding a matching amount from his own funds to ensure that he will be careful not to lose the envelope. If the mark agrees, the shill produces an envelope, into which he places the money in front of both the victim and the con man. The mark may not have enough money, in which case he may make a trip to the bank to make a withdrawal. This game, in earlier years, had to be worked only during banking hours, but today, with the common use of electronic teller machines, is possible at all hours of the day or night.

Both the con man and his shill watch the victim start to place the envelope in his pocket. The con man snatches the envelope back from the mark, telling him that the safest place to keep it is inside his shirt, and in the process opens his shirt and puts the envelope inside, as if to demonstrate the proper carry. This is where he makes the switch. Inside his shirt is another envelope, filled only with paper cut to size. He hands this envelope to the victim, who then places it inside his own shirt. The con man asks the victim for his address, so that he may recover his money later, thanks the victim for his help, and leaves to have his night on the town. The confederate says his farewell and leaves shortly thereafter. Sooner or later, when the con man does not show up, the victim opens the envelope to find he has been taken.

THE MURPHY MAN

In this swindle, which is most suitable for use in a large city with many out-of-town visitors, the "Murphy" man approaches a visitor and suggests that he can get him a woman for the night. Posing as a pimp, he quotes a price to the victim, and asks for the money in advance. The victim pays him, and the con man leads his mark to a hotel. Asking his victim to wait for him outside, or in the lobby, the Murphy man says that he will go upstairs to conclude the deal with the woman and to assure that she is free for the night. He then leaves by another exit. To reassure the victim, he may even tell him the room number, and instruct him to come up after ten minutes.

THE GOPHER SWINDLE

This requires a con man and an assistant. The con man, well-dressed, appears at a hotel, restaurant, or gas station, and asks where the men's room is. He returns a few minutes later, telling the clerk he has lost a very valuable piece of jewelry, and asking his assistance in searching for it. The clerk accompanies the con man, and together they search the premises to try to find the lost jewelry.[4] They fail, and the con man tells the clerk the jewelry is very valuable and he'll pay a substantial reward for its return. Pleading urgent business, he leaves, but gives his business card to the clerk.

Sometime later, the accomplice comes up to the clerk, shows him a piece of jewelry which matches the description of the missing item, and claims he found it on the floor. The clerk tells him it was lost, and that he knows the owner. The finder refuses to give up the jewelry, claiming "finders keepers." At this point, in the belief that he'll still earn a good amount of money from the transaction, he offers the finder a price, the finder accepts, and hands over the item. Anticipating a large profit, the clerk telephones the number on the business card, to find it is a fake.

THE FLOP GAME

In this old con, a shabbily dressed person collapses on the street during rush hour. A well-dressed man, claiming to be a doctor, approaches and examines the person, around whom a crowd has gathered.[5] The victim starts to speak, claiming to be out of a job, not eaten for three days, and having small children at home to whom he or she has given the last of the food. The doctor announces to the crowd that it is a disgrace that, in the richest country in the world, anyone should starve. He takes off his hat, drops a large bill into it, and passes it around for contributions from the onlookers. After the bystanders have made their contributions, the "doctor" thanks them, helps the victim up and says he will help him or her get home.

THE CARD GAME SWINDLE

There are several variants on this old and successful swindle.[6] The con men rent a room at a hotel that is hosting a convention, start a card game, and invite some of the conventioneers to join. The con men explain that, because of local ordinances against gambling, money cannot appear on the table, and the players must buy chips from one of them. They have a cash box, from which they take chips and into which they deposit the money.

In one variant, one of the con men pretends to become violently ill, and the other con men offer to take him back to his room, telling the marks to watch the cash box carefully. They do not return, having at some point during the session emptied the money or switched cash boxes.

In another version, the game is interrupted by the entry of "detectives," who claim to be from the bunco squad and who inform the marks that they are about to be taken by professional gamblers running a crooked game. They handcuff the con men, pick up the cash box, and leave, explaining to the marks the cash box is evidence but as they are innocent parties, they can claim their money at the police station the next day. The fake policemen leave with their prisoners and the victims have lost their money.

THE GOLD BRICK

This one is "old enough to have whiskers" but presumably it or a variation on the theme is still in use. The con man offers to sell the sucker a gold brick. To allay suspicion, the con man advises the sucker to have the ingot assayed, and in doing so the sucker finds out the metal is genuine. He pays the con man for it, and at some point during the proceedings the con man or an accomplice make the switch, substituting an ingot of base metal for the gold one.[7] Sometimes, the con man switches the bricks before consummating the deal, and in other instances when the mark is staying at a hotel, he lets himself into the victim's room with a passkey and makes the switch then.

THE SECURITY SWINDLE

This is a game the con man can play with many different pieces of merchandise. In one case, the item is a violin.[8] The swindler comes into a store, gas station, or other business, and buys a small item. He repeats this a few times, to become known to the proprietor. He then tells the businessman that he is broke, and asks if he can leave his watch, his violin, or other valuables as security for another small purchase. If the proprietor agrees, the con man leaves the piece. For this to succeed, the item left for security must be left out in plain sight by the proprietor, perhaps hanging on the wall or in a display case.

Some days later, the con man's helper, dressed very well, comes into the place of business. He sees the item, and asks how much the proprietor wants for it. The sucker explains that it is not his to sell, as it was left for security by a customer. The accomplice tells the mark this is a very valuable item, and that he'll offer a large sum of money for it if the person who left it abandons the item. He leaves a business card, and departs. Later, the con man returns with his tale of woe. He lost his job, or cannot find a job, and is desperate. He asks the patsy if he would be willing to buy the item from him, as he cannot redeem it. He asks what seems a low price for it, but actually is much more than it is worth. The businessman, calculating that he'll make a handsome profit, accepts the deal and pays what the con man asks. When he tries to get in touch with the well-dressed potential buyer, he finds that he cannot, because the card is a fake.

PANHANDLING

Panhandlers have been around for centuries, sometimes known by other names such as beggars, bums, and tramps. Many of them are simply down-and-outers, who beg for coins to buy a meal, and usually spend it on cheap wine. There are some who earn very good incomes, however, because they have systematized their panhandling so that it is almost a science. One very successful panhandler allegedly had a home in a wealthy suburb of New York, and a wife and children who believed that he was a well-to-do-stockbroker. Each day, he would drive into Manhattan in his Cadillac and park it in a midtown garage, where he would remove his business suit and put on shabby clothes that he kept in the trunk of his car. He then would go out on the streets, having learned from experience which were the best locations. He had his approach well worked out, and from long practice, could intuitively select subjects who would be susceptible to his begging. He would collect a coin or two from each one. None of the people he approached would give him a significant amount of money, but the key to his technique was that he made many "scores" each hour. During an eight-hour day, he would collect as much as if he had actually been working as a stockbroker. At the end of each day, he would return to the garage where he had parked his car, change into his suit, and drive home to his family in Westchester.[9]

There are many variations on the panhandling theme. Another type is the well dressed man who approaches his victim in an embarrassed manner and claims to be a businessman from out of town who has overspent and is now out of money, or who has been robbed.[10] He has no cash or credit cards, and no money to wire or phone his company or relatives for help. If the sucker bites, he'll lend the con man a substantial sum of money.

Another variant is for the well-dressed "businessman" to make the rounds in an office building, explaining that he is in town on a business trip and admitting that he had too much to drink the night before, and was robbed while intoxicated. This sympathy story will get him many "loans" from credulous victims.

THE INTENTIONAL VICTIM

This theme covers a lot of ground, the object of the fraud being to set someone else up for a lawsuit. One type, well-known to insurance companies, is the "leg-breaker," the person who is "accidentally" hit by a car, or who breaks a leg "accidentally" in a building. Working in collaboration with a lawyer, who is usually part of the swindle, the "victim" becomes the plaintiff in a lawsuit. The physical injury is, in the view of the swindler, a cheap price to pay for the large settlement that usually results.

One reason for the proliferation of "whiplash" claims in recent years is this sort of injury is very hard to disprove, and so there is no need for a fraud artist to sustain a severe physical injury or secure the cooperation of an unethical doctor.

Insurance companies are very much aware of this type of swindle, and employ staffs of investigators to verify the claims against them. One of their most valuable tools is a file of the names of people who have brought suit before, which cues them to those who make a career of injury claims. While it is true that a "flop artist" can assume a new identity for the next "job," an investigation can often reveal whether or not the claimant's identity is genuine.

Another variant on the lawsuit theme is to set up a businessman for a lawsuit for false arrest. In its simplest form, the con artist enters a store which he knows employs private detectives to counter shoplifters. He behaves furtively, and pretends to slip merchandise into his pockets. When he's sure that he has attracted the attention of one of the staff, he heads for an exit. An accomplice remains nearby, to serve as a "witness." When the detective arrests him, the con man protests his innocence, and makes a scene, being careful to keep his protest verbal and non-violent. He refuses to submit to a search, and the store detective sends for the police to lodge a formal complaint. When the police arrive, and place the "shoplifter" under arrest and search him, they find no evidence on him. With his case fortified by his "witness," the con man can either sue or accept a settlement out of court.

As with personal injury cases, insurance companies keep detailed files of the plaintiffs, and freely exchange information for mutual protection. This is one reason a person who applies for a policy, or makes a claim against an insurance company, will have his name in the files of many, or in a central bureau. This practice has led to apprehension about "Big Brotherism" and the files kept on honest citizens. The reason for the extensive record keeping is innocuous, merely a self-protection measure by the insurance companies.

Yet another method of setting up a merchant for a false arrest suit is for the con man to buy a valuable piece of merchandise, for example a watch, and pay for it by check. He then goes into the shop next door and tries to sell it, usually for far less than he paid for it. He suggests the proprietor check on the value of the watch with the jeweler next door. The jeweler becomes suspicious, and confronts his client, demanding to know why he is trying to sell a watch he has just bought, thinking the client bought the watch with a bad check and is now trying to get rid of it. The "client" feeds his suspicion, saying that he changed his mind about needing a watch. The jeweler asks for the watch back, and the con man refuses, further inflaming the jeweler's suspicion. At this point, the jeweler sends for the police, and an arrest ensues. The police investigation discloses that the check the con man gave the jeweler was valid, and that sets the scene for a false arrest suit.[11]

THE RICH LADY SWINDLE

An elegant and well-dressed lady buys a lot of merchandise at a store which carries only top-line items. When it is time to pay she tells the clerk or proprietor she has forgotten her wallet and checkbook, and cannot pay. She suggests that the sucker accompany her home, where she will settle the bill. She says her limousine is outside, and she'll have her chauffer return the mark to the store, to help make up for the inconvenience. They load the merchandise into the car, and drive to a wealthy neighborhood, where they start to get out of the car. The lady hands some of the merchandise to the merchant, filling his arms, and tells him to ring the bell so the maid and butler can help get the rest of the packages inside. As he reaches the doorstep, the merchant hears the car drive off, and he loses the merchandise still in the car.[12]

A SIMPLE MAIL FRAUD

An advertisement appears, offering a coat hanger and a cigarette lighter for a price. The victim mails the money to the address listed, and a few days later receives an envelope containing a match and a nail.[13]

THE FAKE COLLECTION AGENCY

A businessman with long overdue bills answers an advertisement for a collection agency. When he arrives at their office, the "manager" tells him they do not collect their fee until they recover the debt, and their fee is a modest 15%. The businessman agrees, and hands over his delinquent invoices. The manager hands him some legal papers to sign, telling him that they are powers-of-attorney and authorization forms. When the businessman has signed them, the manager tells him he will have the papers notarized and filed with the authorities the same day, and asks the businessman for the required fees, which are modest. Upon receiving the fees, the manager sends one of his subordinates out to have the papers processed.

As the weeks go by, the businessman, if he inquires, will hear from the manager that the agency is still working on the debts, and that they expect results soon. One day, he finds that the phone is disconnected, and a visit to the "office" tells him that the occupants have moved, leaving no forwarding address.

The confidence ring has been systematically collecting "filing fees" from all who sought its services, and the large number of clients paid sums that added up to a substantial amount.[14]

THE INVESTMENT FRAUD (PONZI SCHEME)

The swindler advertises that he can offer very substantial returns to very modest investors. An investment of five hundred dollars, for example, will yield the investor dividends of one hundred dollars a month. The sucker who answers the ad may think this is too good to be true, but the next month he gets a check in the mail for one hundred dollars. The following month he finds another hundred dollar check in his mailbox. The next month he finds that indeed it was too good to be true, as no check arrives and when he goes to the office of the investment company he finds it empty, with no trace of the occupants.[15]

There are two variants on this swindle:

One is to pay back part of the money invested, still making a profit on the transaction, three hundred dollars in this example.

The other is to make payments to keep the sucker satisfied, not only to allow time to get out of town, but to encourage him to send the con man new clients, offering a bird-dog fee of one hundred dollars for each one. This pyramids the sales, and the con man uses the new investments to pay off the old clients in installments, until he feels he has exhausted the local market.

THE FORTUNE-TELLING SCAM

While many people believe in psychics, fortune tellers, and other "readers" and pay modest sums to get advice and predictions of the future, some are victimized on a large scale by outright con artists. The method is as follows:

The victim visits the gypsy lady, who tells her the root of her misery is money, and she can cleanse herself of her hard luck by destroying some of it in a special ceremony. She instructs the mark to bring a large sum of money on her next visit. When the victim shows up with the money, the gypsy places it in an envelope and chants prayers over it. At some point during the ceremony, she switches the envelope for one containing only pieces of paper cut to the size of the bills. Then she places the envelope in the fire, and says more prayers. At the end of the session, she tells the victim that the evil spirits have been cleansed and her life will be better from now on.

Sometimes the deception involves the victim's jewelry, if the victim is affluent enough to have valuable pieces. The gypsy tells the mark to bring them with her, and she'll keep them for several days and return them cleansed of evil spirits. After several days go by, without the return of the jewels, the victim finds the gypsy has folded her tent and moved on.[16]

SNAKE OIL

Patent medicines have a bad name for some very good reasons. They have been sold at carnivals, by door-to-door salesmen, and in local stores. They are usually useless concoctions, but there is no difficulty in finding people who swear that a certain medicine worked for them, because the human body heals itself in most illnesses, with or without the remedy.

Patent medicines are only one manifestation of the charlatanism that has been a part of health care since prehistoric times, and although government regulations have driven out some of the more blatant snake oil salesmen, who used to award themselves medical degrees to lend authority to their sales pitches, the recent problems with the "starch blockers" shows us the field is not yet closed. We will examine these problems more closely in the chapter on health care.

TOUTS

The tout is a tipster, who passes betting tips to his victims, extracting the promise that they'll split the take with him if it pays off. Touts work at race tracks, betting halls, and even stockbroker's offices, among the clients watching the big board. The tout approaches his victim, starts up a conversation, and soon claims that he is very experienced in the field, or has inside information, and offers to pass on tips to the victim, in return for a promise to split the winnings.

The tout does not have to know very much, as his scam does not depend on any ability to predict winners. He works by making different predictions to different people, knowing that just by the laws of chance, some of his tips will be valid. When one of his winners comes in, he seeks out the person whom he tipped off and collects. Meanwhile, he avoids the losers.

Touts make the round of tracks, betting offices, and financial centers around the country. They can't work a particular locale for long, because of the prospect of an unpleasant confrontation with a victim, or even arrest and prosecution.

THE OLD SCAMS LIVE ON

With this quick survey of classic frauds, we've seen how old ideas linger in the minds of confidence artists, cropping up again and again as each new generation of potential victims arrives. Some of the classics need cosmetic work, to keep up with changing times, but the basics remain the same. Technological innovations dictate some changes, and help bring about new con games and swindles, but the fundamental principles of deception, of preying on the weaknesses of human nature, never change.

NOTES

1. *Short Cons,* Scot Tinker, Eden Press, 1977.
2. Ibid. p. 5.
3. Ibid. p. 6.
4. Ibid. p. 26.
5. Ibid. p. 27.
6. Ibid. p. 34.
7. *The Bunco Book,* Walter B. Gibson, 1976, p. 4.
8. Ibid. p. 5.
9. Related to author by a professional panhandler.
10. *Bunco Book,* p. 10.
11. Ibid. p. 22.
12. Ibid. p. 25.
13. Related to author in elementary school by a teacher who was near retirement age. This one is old!
14. *Bunco Book,* p. 68.
15. Ibid. p. 70.
16. Ibid. p. 72.

ADVERTISING FRAUDS

Most of us are familiar with the petty deceptions and outright lies that many advertisers use routinely. We've been exposed to the many commercials on television that promise us we will be sexier or happier if we use a certain cosmetic, drink a certain brand of beer, or buy some other product. This constant exposure desensitizes us to exaggerated claims somewhat, and we often simply don't respond to the claims. In fact, many advertisers are distressed that TV watchers use commercial breaks to go the bathroom or kitchen.

There are some flagrant frauds on TV, most of which operate only for short times, until the slow-moving mechanism of law enforcement catches up to them. Most of us have seen commercials for overpriced items available by calling an 800 number displayed on the screen, and realize we can buy the same or better quality products for less at local stores.

A recent variant is diet pills, supposedly with newly discovered ingredients, which are guaranteed to work. The wording of the guarantee is the interesting part, and the crux of the scheme. The viewer can, by calling an 800 number, obtain a supply of the diet pills for twenty dollars. If he is not satisfied with the results, the vendor will give him another supply of pills, at no cost, providing he pays the handling and shipping, which comes to about three dollars. The pills are the same that sell for about three dollars in drugstores and supermarkets. The initial purchase earns the advertiser a huge profit, and subsequent sales give him the normal profit enjoyed by retail outlets.

We learn from experience that most advertising claims are lies of one sort or another, sometimes outright criminal frauds and other times based on unproven assumptions regarding certain trendy products or substances.

About twenty five years ago, a small company in New York added shoe polishing cloths containing "silicon" to its line of notions. The claim was that the "silicon" contained in the cloth would help obtain a higher shine. In fact, the cloth strips were simply trimmings from the material used for ironing board covers, which would have gone out with the trash otherwise. This material has a hard, silver finish on one side, and a soft backing on the other. The soft backing did indeed work well in shining shoes.[1]

Buying goods sight unseen is a risky practice. It's not necessary to go into great detail and enumerate the instances in which shoddy merchandise sells through TV or other advertisements which do not allow the buyer to inspect the goods in person. While there are honest mail-order houses which have established reputations for fair dealing over a long time, there are also fly-by-night operators with compelling offers that seem too good to miss. These are the ones which offer the greatest risk.

NOTES

1. Personal knowledge of the author, who in his youth worked at this company for three months. The vice president, an affable man, admitted to the author that the claim of "silicon" was a "gimmick."

BUSINESS FRAUDS

While all frauds involve some sort of business, some are especially aimed at companies, where they take advantage of inefficiencies in the people themselves and some loopholes in the law.

The simplest business fraud is the fake invoice. This piece of idiocy should never work, but it does often enough to make it worthwhile. The fraud artist makes up a company name and establishes a bank account in that name. He orders invoices printed, picks up the Yellow Pages, and sends invoices for nonexistent deliveries and services to the companies he culls from the directory.

Theoretically, this should never work. In companies which have even a rudimentary accounting system, staffed by conscientious people, it doesn't. Each delivery or service call is documented, with a receiving ticket written up and stapled to the packing slip or service slip, a copy of the ticket going to the person authorizing the purchase and another to accounting, where a clerk vouches it against the original purchase order. The purchase order is the key, and companies which have, and enforce, a strict rule that every procurement must have a purchase order signed by the individual authorized to do so, will not be vulnerable to this scam.

Often, however, especially in small companies, there is no system, and it's impossible to tell from any available paperwork which are legitimate invoices and which are bogus ones. A harried, overworked clerk issues a check and passes it on to the executive whose signature is authorized. Often, the executive will sign anything he finds before him, assuming that if the check is already made out it must be legitimate. This lack of internal controls leaves the company wide open to the fake invoice.[1]

A step up from the fake invoice is the fake service call. This ploy takes advantage of the fact that even in well-run-companies, service calls often don't have purchase orders to authorize them, or else have a "blanket purchase order" issued to cover them. American business, like the Government, is flooded with paperwork and the blanket purchase order or other informal arrangement is an attempt to reduce the paperwork load by eliminating the formality of a purchase order for routine items. Moreover, authorization of a service call does not usually go through the usual channels, with a written requisition passed to the purchasing agent, who then arranges for the work to be ordered. A typist may contact the typewriter repair company for a service call, without being required to clear it with the purchasing agent, the comptroller, or any other executive.

The con man, armed with a pad of service call tickets, arrives at the office and tells the receptionist that he's there to service the typewriter, for example. The receptionist, upon checking with other people in the office, finds nobody who called for service. The "service man" then requests that the receptionist sign a service ticket, purely as a formality so that he could justify his time to his supervisor. He hands her a carbon of the ticket, and leaves.

The ticket is also an invoice, and some days later a copy arrives in the mail. Printed on it is a minimum charge, which applies whether there is any work performed or not. If the accounting clerk phones to question the invoice, the con man, who has established an office or who works out of his home, answers that someone made a service call and he has a signature on his ticket to document it.[2] Of course, the matter would not stand up to close investigation, but as the amount on the invoice is usually small, there rarely is any follow-up and the company usually pays.

A more involved business fraud is called the "bust-out." Although simple in principle it is difficult to execute, and often takes weeks or months to carry out. The first point is for the con man to acquire control of a business, which can come about in a number of ways. A businessman who has a weakness for gambling, for example, is open to having a con man take control of his company to settle a large debt. Another way is to buy an existing company on a short term loan. The key is the company must have either a large inventory or an excellent credit rating. If there is a loan involved in the buyout, selling the inventory at cut-rate prices will raise the money to pay off the loan. Otherwise, the company's credit rating is helpful in acquiring a large quantity of merchandise to sell off quickly.

Basically, the system of profiting from a bust-out is to use the company to purchase as much stock of goods as the creditors will allow, selling it quickly, and then either leaving town or declaring bankruptcy.[3]

In the "bust-out" there is usually a front man, called a "pencil," an honest executive who is not in on the fraud. He is the one who runs the routine operations of the company while the fraud artist concentrates his efforts on the scam. The "pencil" is also the one whose feet will be in the fire after the fraud artist leaves town and he'll have a hard time proving he was not party to the scheme.

The mechanics of a bust-out can be very elaborate, depending on the imagination and resources of the con man. If organized crime is involved, there will be a group of "legitimate" companies taking part.

One of the myths of the Twentieth Century is that those involved in organized crime sometimes decide to "go straight," investing their criminal proceeds in "legitimate" business. In reality, they establish a "legitimate" source of income to satisfy the **IRS, for laundering money, and as receivers of illegitimate goods.**

Such a company can buy goods sold at a low price during a bust-out and resell them at a large profit. In fact, a fraud artist who is connected with organized crime can use a bust-out to supply his "legitimate" company at very low prices, enabling it to beat the competition.

The end of the game can come two ways: The con man can simply leave town after having extracted as much as he could from the purchase and quick sales of inventory. The appropriate moment is when the vendors are unwilling to supply any more goods on credit and begin pressing for payment of the debts.

The other way is to declare bankruptcy. To support this, it's necessary to have the proper invoices, bills of sale, and other paperwork to support the transactions, as the bankruptcy court will be interested in the events that led to the bankruptcy. There are several ingenious means of disposing of the money, and their success depends on the imagination of the con man, as well as on luck.

NOTES

1. *Classic Mail Frauds,* Scot Tinker, Eden Press, 1977, p. 12.
2. *Clipping The Flocks,* Scot Tinker, Eden Press, 1977, pp. 27-28.
3. *Big Time Operator's Manual,* Scot Tinker, Eden Press, 1977, p. 14, pp. 38-39.

CHAIN LETTERS AND PYRAMIDS

Almost everyone has gotten a chain letter at one time. The chain letter urges the reader to send a dollar, or some other sum of money, to the name at the top of a list, then retype the letter, deleting the top name and adding his own at the bottom. The letter promises riches to the people who follow the plan. As Carey and Sherman so carefully calculate in their book,[1] the chain soon snowballs to involve a fantastic number of people, and only the originators of the chain letter stand a decent chance of making any money.

The principle of the chain letter is that of the pyramid, with a small top and large base. All money flows towards the top, and the people on the bottom, in reality, are the payors, not the collectors.

As we shall see, there are many fraud schemes built upon the principle of the pyramid. Referral sales schemes, in which the buyer hears that he'll get his water softener or other merchandise free if he steers enough of his friends to the salesman, are a good example.

Another is pyramid sales, in which the major effort is to build up a network of "dealers," rather than selling the goods to the public. As in all pyramid schemes, the bubble eventually bursts because there are only a certain number of people and the scheme, which depends on continued growth, collapses when the limit is reached.

NOTES

1. *A Compendium of Bunk,* Carey and Sherman 1976, Charles C. Thomas. pp. 48-55.

DOOR TO DOOR

There are legitimate door to door sales companies, among them **Fuller Brush and Avon. There are also many sleazy, fly-by-night outfits that peddle fraud.**

For years, legitimate street salesmen have sold their goods to householders in a more or less honest manner. While some of them did practice dishonesty, most of those representing a legitimate company gave the customers what they purchased. The prices were somewhat higher than prices for similar items in stores because of the commission system. Most people aren't aware that street salesmen earn from twenty five to fifty percent commissions.

There were some instances of fakers impersonating salesmen for reputable companies, taking orders and accepting deposits, and never returning. Most fraud artists, however, were interested in more than the small "take" from this sort of operation.

In the small league there are also those who go from door to door pretending to be collecting money for one charity or another. Sometimes the charity does not exist, other times the charity is real, and the credentials stolen, or forged.

All of these street salesmen (and women, too!) first have to get the victim to open the door. Sometimes the enticement is a "free gift," and at other times it is the offer of a "free" demonstration. The salesman may elicit sympathy by stating that he gets paid for just giving demonstrations, which is an outright lie. Sometimes, the salesman will tell his intended victim that he'll qualify for a discount if he allows him to make a demonstration. This, too, is part of the con.[1]

There are several tired old schemes for selling goods door to door, but new ones pop up every year. The old vacuum cleaner pitch, in which the salesman dumps a bag of dust and sweepings on the floor at the first opportunity, then comes in and cleans up the mess with the new vacuum cleaner, has been done very often, and it's still offensive.

Often, as in freezer food plans, there is a deceptive pitch regarding the money to be saved by buying frozen food with the plan offered. The plan involves, of course, buying a freezer at an inflated price. As this is the object of the whole exercise, the salesman tells the customer that he can drop out of the plan at any time he becomes dissatisfied. He glosses over the point that the customer is stuck for the freezer. Many customers do drop out when they find they are not getting lower food prices with the plan.

Another piece of hardware that keeps selling is the water softener, especially in areas of the country that have hard water. The salesman, often with an appointment made for him by a "boiler room" operation, arrives and launches into an hour long pitch regarding the perils of untreated water. He'll open up a large case containing laboratory glassware and vials of chemicals, and "prove" to the homeowner that he's ruining his plumbing and risking his health by allowing untreated water to flow through his pipes. There may be some special enticements, such as an "introductory discount," or a referral plan to allow him to get his water softener free by steering the salesman to his friends, but in the end the victim signs a contract for a water softener at a price higher than he would have paid at a local store. Add to this installation charges which are also inflated, and the cost of a credit contract, and the homeowner spends as much as fifteen hundred dollars for something which would cost him three locally.

Water softener salesman hand out "lifetime" guarantees, knowing they won't honor them, as the "company" will fold its tent and move on shortly.

Such salesmen tend to push trendy items, closely following the fads in the media. For the last few years, "solar" and other energy saving devices have been pushed hard. Twenty years ago, the trend was nuclear bomb shelters and allied equipment. Many backyard "contractors" set themselves up as "experts" on shelters, just as today out-of-work plumbers put together simple and cheap arrays of pipes and tanks and sell them as "solar" water heaters, promising the homeowner will recuperate the inflated prices quickly through savings on his utility bills, a claim which is impossible to check out until it's too late.

There is now some protection for the victim of an unscrupulous salesman. Some states have laws providing for a "cooling off period," usually several days, during which the buyer can think over the contract he signed and, if he changes his mind, annul it by notifying the company.

Some salesmen still use the blank contract trick, offering the customer a blank form to sign and telling him that he'll fill it in later, at the office. The excuses for this vary, but they still work on people who are not careful.

It's in the field of home improvements and repairs that the con artists really hit hard. Some of them even impersonate public officials, such as building "inspectors." One group passed themselves off as "termite inspectors" for the city, and inveigled victims into paying for the extermination of termites that were allegedly infesting their homes.[2]

A particularly brazen duo claimed to be gas company repairmen trying to trace a "gas leak." They rang the bell and asked for permission to enter the yard to check the pipes. Starting a small fire, they quickly put it out and told the householder that the house was unsafe for occupancy. While in the house, they stole a wallet and some money that had been in a hiding place in the refrigerator.[3]

Fake "inspectors" have persuaded many homeowners they needed work on their septic tanks, roofs, plumbing, wiring and heating systems. One bold scam was the "furnace inspector" who gained access to the house on the pretense of "inspecting" the furnace. After disassembling the furnace, he told the homeowner it was in a dangerous condition, and that he suggested buying a new furnace. Of course, he was willing to suggest from whom he should buy it. If the householder refused to buy a new furnace, the "inspector" left the old one in pieces on the floor of the basement.

The "inspector" ploy is very effective if the victim is not too bright, and credulous when the "inspector" reinforces his sales pitch with the threat of a fine. With the threat of a large fine hanging over him, the homeowner is relieved when the "inspector" tells him that if he gets the defect fixed immediately, he won't report it. By coincidence, the "inspector" has a friend in the business who can perform an immediate repair. This ploy works especially among sophisticated city people, because they are so accustomed to "shakedowns" by public officials they are relieved this "inspector" does not ask for a bribe, but on the contrary seems to be going out of his way to be helpful.[4]

Fraudulant roof repairs and driveway blacktopping are still with us. One variation used is the "leftover" ploy. The workman rings the bell and informs whomever answers that he just finished a job down the street and has enough material left over to "waterproof" the roof or driveway. To avoid the nuisance of hauling it back to the yard, he'll let the homeowner have it for far less than he'd normally pay. The price is right, but the material is cheap, often being just used motor oil for the driveway blacktopping. The workman collects his money, and when the first rain comes the oil washes off.[5]

A big ticket item in home repairs is the aluminum siding fraud. The sales pitch can be very high-pressure, with the salesman claiming to have a "special introductory offer" to push him into signing. Some will use the referral sales pitch, telling the victim that he'll get a certain amount back from each additional sale if he allows his house to be used as a "demonstrator." In some extreme cases, the salesman will tell the customer, if the price seems to be more than he can afford, that he'll lend him the money for the initial payment out of his own pocket to get the order. He then has the customer sign a credit contract, which makes it a three-party deal and enables the salesman to collect his money immediately and earn a commission on the contract from the credit company, and leaves the householder with long-term payments.

Similar tactics prevail in sales of other home "improvements," such as swimming pools and remodeling projects. Although the work may be honest, and the materials sound, the sales tactics tend to be high-pressure, and often cross over the line into fraud.

NOTES

1. *Fraud Investigation,* Glick and Newsom, Charles C. Thomas, 1974.

2. *Clipping The Flocks,* Scot Tinker, Eden Press, 1977, p. 8.

3. *A Compendium of Bunk,* Carey and Sherman, Charles C. Thomas, 1976, p. 60.

4. *Clipping The Flocks,* pp. 8-11. *Compendium,* p. 42.

5. *Clipping The Flocks,* p. 12.

DRUG "BURNS"

Keeping in mind the ease and enthusiasm with which fraud artists prey on ordinary citizens, it is not surprising they also prey on each other. One extremely profitable, and extremely dangerous, way in which they do this is in narcotics deals. When a supplier of a contraband drug offers to supply a dealer or a wholesaler with a large amount, the opportunity to make a large profit very quickly exists, and the opportunity to make an even larger one by supplying a worthless substitute is tempting.

This practice has become so common that a special term for it exists in our language, the "drug burn." "Burning" a buyer by substituting lactose or talcum powder for heroin, for example, is one way in which the seller can attempt to cheat the buyer. Another is by excessive dilution.

It is an old saying that there is honor among thieves, but this widely accepted dictum is almost always false. Those who prey on the public have no inhibitions about preying on each other, if the opportunity exists and if they think they can succeed. On drug deals, there are roughly two types of "burns."

The first is to substitute a counterfeit substance for the drug. This is why large contraband drug dealers now use chemical tests to assay the authenticity or purity of the substance at the time of the buy. There are available small and portable test kits, usually sold to police, for this purpose. While these were originally conceived for the use of drug enforcement squads, the companies who make them are under no legal requirement to sell them only to police agencies, and many of them find their way into the hands of drug dealers and wholesalers.

The larger dealers, who buy quantities worth hundreds of thousands of dollars at a time, often employ their own chemists, who come to the site of the exchange and test the questioned substance on the spot.

The other variant is the outright "ripoff," in which the dealer or distributor attempts to take possession of the drug without paying for it. This crosses the line between fraud and robbery.

The prospect of suffering huge losses in dishonest deals results in the participants in illegal drug buys coming armed, and often a shootout occurs when the deal "goes down." This accounts for a certain proportion of the corpses that turn up shot to death with no witnesses. Such murders are difficult to solve, as the connection between the victim and his killer is clandestine.

On a smaller scale, the dealer often attempts to cheat his addict clientele by diluting the drug beyond the usual amount. He knows the addict lacks the recourse that the victim in other frauds has, that of reporting him to the police.

Without getting too far afield, it is worth noting that "burns" and "ripoffs" occur in other illegal transactions, such as "fencing" stolen goods, and that contraband is not limited to controlled drugs, but also includes currency, gold, diamonds, and other smuggled items. These transactions can also lead to violence, but much more rarely than those involving drugs.

ENTRAPMENT

Any involvement with sex or romance offers the fraud artist an opportunity to defraud a victim. Lonely hearts clubs and Murphy men victimize lonely people. For the most direct and blatant fraud, falling short only of an actual hold-up, the "badger game" stands out.

In its prototypical form, the badger game requires a man and a woman working in concert. The woman allows herself to be "picked up" by a man. Any man will do, but if he's a married man on a business trip, seeking a little excitement outside his marital relationship, he's a prime candidate.

After the pick-up, the couple goes to the woman's lodging. When they're comfortably and compromisingly between the sheets, the male partner of the fraud duo comes in, pretending to be the woman's husband. Quite expectedly, a row ensues, with the "husband" angrily denouncing both his "wife" and her lover. During the discussion, the "husband" threatens to notify the police, or the John's wife, further raising the level of anxiety. This sets the stage for a "settlement." Sometimes prompted by the "wife," the mark offers the husband money to soothe his hurt feelings. If the mark is lucky, that's the end of it.[1]

There are several variants on this scheme. If the mark is married, he's very open to blackmail, and the payments may last a long time and involve a large sum of money. Another angle is the compromising letters variant, in which no physical contact need take place and which can be run by one man. The con artist places ads in lonely hearts and "swinger's" publications, claiming to be a single woman seeking a good time. When the replies come in, he answers in an enticing manner, and sooner or later collects some letters from married men who have been foolish enough to put their desires for illicit relationships on paper. Depending on his resourcefulness, the con artist can trace some of these potential victims, even if they use post office boxes for their contacts. At this point, he can pretend to be either an outraged husband who has discovered his "wife's" compromising mail, or an outright blackmailer, who threatens to show the letters to the victim's wife unless he pays him for silence.

Another variant is for one or more men to burst into the room when the couple is in a compromising position, pretending to be police or private detectives. This variant works when the couple go to a hotel, where it is unlikely that the "husband" would have a key to the premises. The "private detectives" claim that they have been **hired by the woman's husband, and they may even take photographs upon entry.**

If they claim to be the police, they may claim to be from the vice squad, enforcing the law against illicit sex. There may or may not be an applicable law in the state in which a particular badger game runs, but if the victim is from out of state he will be unaware of this. In fact, some states still have archaic laws pertaining to sexual conduct.

Yet another variant on this scheme is the "underage girl" ploy. This requires that the fraud artist work in concert with a teenage girl who looks older than she is. The "police detective" bursts into the room and threatens to arrest the mark for relations with a minor. The girl tearfully reveals that she is under the age of consent, and the stage is set for extortion.

Yet another tactic is for the female partner in this game to be of legal age, but able to pass for younger. If the "pickup" occurs in a bar, the mark will assume that she's old enough, as operators of bars are forbidden to serve alcohol to minors and usually are careful in checking customer's ages. When the "detective" bursts in, he claims the lady's driver's license or other proof of age is forged, or stolen, and that she's really a minor. As sexual relations with a minor is a felony in all states, often falling under the law regarding child molesting, the mark has good cause to worry.

A variant about which we hear little is the homosexual one. Most states have laws pertaining to "unnatural acts," "crimes against nature," or "sodomy," and although these are not usually enforced when the relationship involves consenting adults, they are still on the books and ready for use when the act takes place outside a private home or apartment.

57

The victim may be either an overt homosexual or a married man with a secret life who indulges when away from home. While the married man has the most to fear, since he usually does not want this dark side of his personality revealed to his wife or employer, it's a mistake to assume that the hardened homosexual is invulnerable.

Sexual relations with a minor are also illegal when the contact is homosexual, and the man who picks up a male who later turns out to be "underage" is open to felony prosecution. Because of the highly emotional nature of popular attitudes towards sexual misconduct, and especially sex with a minor, penalties are likely to be severe. Combine that with homosexuality and we have a truly threatening combination.

The fake rape is another variation of the badger theme. The "rape" can be statutory or violent. In its simplest form, it doesn't even require more than the female, who allows herself to be picked up. In the car, or in the room, she tears her clothing, dishevels her hair, and claims that she'll call the police and charge the mark with rape, unless he pays her. She may play the role of a casual pickup, and then demand money, or she may play the outright prostitute and demand, instead of the agreed fee for service, the entire contents of the victim's wallet.[2]

She may, after consummation of the act, claim to be underage, and demand payment in return for silence. It's obvious that this theme can have both hetero- and homosexual versions. Whatever the form, the badger game, calculated to cause the victim to panic, works very well and fraud artists who play the badger game find new victims for this old trick every day.

NOTES

1. *Clipping The Flocks,* Scot Tinker, Eden Press, 1977, p. 15.
2. A fellow employee of the author, when both were working the police beat for a newspaper, picked up a young lady who was hitchhiking. Shortly after she entered the car, she tore her clothing and informed the driver that she was going to scream "rape." The

driver had good presence of mind, and pulled into the parking lot of the police station, which was nearby, and told her to scream all she wished. He explained to her that he was acquainted with most of the members of the police force, and that the likely result was that she would be arrested. This is a rare example of total failure of the badger game, caused by a combination of a cool and calculating mind and good fortune. Most intended victims don't fare as well.

It doesn't always end so well. Sometimes, the victim can't go to the police because the fraud artist is the police. There is a small minority of crooked cops who "shake down" their victims, threatening them with arrest unless they pay up. This happens mainly in vice and gambling investigations. However, in some of the better-run police departments, there is hope for the courageous victim, if he reports the incident to the "internal affairs" department, which is the section of the police that polices the policemen. They investigate the alleged wrongdoing, and the result is not always a whitewash.

FLEECING RELATIVES

In some con games, the victim is not the target, but a relative or neighbor, or even a friend, is. The target is merely the lever the con man uses to pry money loose from the victim.

One simple con is the "dead man's debt." Scanning the obituaries, the con man works up a list of recently deceased people and the addresses of their survivors. He approaches the relatives, claiming that the deceased had borrowed money from him but died before he could repay the loan. Although this con is old, it still works.

A variant on this is the C.O.D. racket. The con artist, posing as a delivery man, brings a package to the widow, son, or other survivor at the same address as the deceased. He claims the deceased had ordered the goods. Acting surprised and sympathetic, he collects the money and runs.

The C.O.D. racket also works with living persons. The phoney delivery man brings a package when the addressee is not home, and leaves it with the wife, other relative, or even a neighbor, of course collecting the C.O.D. charge.

Modern technology makes it possible for the con man to work some variants of this racket at long distance. One type who victimizes people by remote control is called the "sheet writer." He works by frequenting hotels and resorts, striking up conversations with guests. Whether tourists or conventioneers, they are vulnerable to the sheet writer, who during the course of the conversation asks many friendly and seemingly harmless questions. He'll ask if the victim is married, the names of his wife and children, and many other details in a manner which will not seem probing but will flesh out the frame of the acquaintance. His manner will be flattering and friendly, and perhaps he'll reveal that his home is not too far from his target's. In parting, he'll of course ask for his target's name and address, promising to phone or visit when he returns home.

Armed with this information, he wires the target's wife or business associate. Tersely, the telegram explains that he lost all of his money through a mishap, mentions some personal details to authenticate the request (your middle name is Helen, your mother lives in Council Bluffs) and asks for additional funds to be wired. The basis of this trick is that the target supposedly lost his wallet, and therefore cannot supply official documentation to identify himself, as is normal procedure when receiving "Moneygrams." He asks that the sender instruct the telegraph company to require the collector of the money to give a piece of personal information, which he already knows from requesting the target. This enables the con man to collect and cash the wired check without proper I.D.[1]

There are many variants on this basic ploy. The con man may not always pose as a friendly acquaintance, but instead identify himself as a writer doing a story on the convention, a public relations executive for the hotel, etc. This semi-official role-playing will often open up people who otherwise would not be inclined to be friendly and discuss themselves. Again, without seeming to probe, he elicits personal details. Among the important details are the name and address of the nearest relative, or the business associate, along with the phone number.

Choosing a moment when the target is away from the hotel, in case the relative decides to check by telephoning, the con man rings the number. He explains that he's a bail bondsman, that the target has been arrested on a relatively minor charge, and that he needs several hundred dollars to arrange bail. The con man adds that the target told him to mention some personal details, such as the names of the children or pets, to indicate that the request is authentic.[2]

This maneuver enables the con man to receive payment under his own identity, or any for which he has official documentation. Using this technique, he can collect several thousands of dollars in one day or evening.

NOTES

1. *Clipping The Flocks,* Scot Tinker, Eden Press, 1977, P.O. Box

8410, Fountain Valley, CA 92708. p. 31. Also, *Short Cons,* Scot Tinker, Eden Press, p. 9.

2. *Short Cons,* p. 28.

GAMBLING DANGERS

Gambling is an interesting pastime for some, an addiction for others. It's a way for some to earn a lot of money quickly, and to lose a lot quickly for others. Gambling among equals has its hazards. Luck can cause one to win, and the other to lose, sometimes quite heavily. This is normal, and it's obvious that gambling for more than an affordable amount is poor practice. A "friendly" game can turn into a disaster.

Gambling in a commercial, above-board gambling establishment has its problems, too. Obviously, a racetrack or a casino is set up to earn money, and the odds always favor the house. For example, the games in a casino pay off at slightly less than true odds, so the casino gets its six percent (usually) "off the top." At a race track, the parimutuel system is set up so that in effect the players are betting against each other, not the track. The payoffs are always less than the amount of money wagered and the track takes its fee off the top before paying off. The commercial establishments are usually honest, in the sense that the odds and payoffs are known to the players, and there are security precautions against cheating either by players or dishonest employees. This is necessary because any suspicion of dishonest practice can damage the reputation of a casino or track, and reduce business. Commercial gambling establishments are also monitored by a government agency, usually a state gambling or racetrack commission, to insure further the honesty of the transactions.

For the individual gambler, the summing-up is that, in honest games with friends, he should break about even in the long run, assuming a normal amount of luck. In playing at commercial establishments, he will lose over the long haul, because the house skims its profit off the top, before assigning payoffs. The games against professional gamblers, however, are another story.

Professional gamblers are a little documented subculture in our country. There is much misinformation about them, and few facts available to the public. There is a myth that some of them are extremely sharp and perceptive players, who by superior skill manage to earn their livings at cards, dice or whatever game they play. It's a safe assumption that there are very few of these, just as there are very few outstanding people in any field.

In reality, the people who earn their livings at gambling do so by cheating, as in any other con game. They are fraud artists, in addition to breaking the law in other respects in states where gambling is illegal.

In some states, the law comes down very hard on gamblers whether honest or not. There have been some instances of church bingo parties running into difficulties with the police. The effect of these laws is usually counterproductive. The laws keep gamblers underground, and they discourage those who have been cheated from complaining to the police because that involves a confession that they were participating in an illegal activity.

Some gambling fraud operators are truly freelance, working alone and depending on their skill at cheating to stack the odds in their favor. More often, however, they work with confederates, who aid in "steering" business their way rather than in the fraud itself.

The classic card swindle is called "three-card monte," and usually works in this manner:

The "game" takes place in an area accessible to the public, where the mark comes across an old man playing with a younger one. The old man shuffles three cards and places them face down. The younger man has to pick the red card from the three. Each try has some money on the table to cover the bet. The younger man picks the correct card every time, which is not surprising, because the corner of the red one is slightly bent. If the mark bites, when he tries to pick the red card he fails every time, because the old man, who's part of the scheme, has switched a black card with a bent corner for the red one.[1]

In this game, the old man may pretend to be drunk, to aid the illusion of incompetence. The younger man is a shill. There may be a third party, seemingly unconnected with the game, to "steer" the victim to the game.

Marked cards are common devices used in cheating. Originally, individual cheaters marked the decks themselves, but in the Twentieth Century marked decks have been manufactured. They are available in novelty shops in many large cities.[2] Playing dice, or "craps" is a daily activity in many communities. If the players know each other, there may be no cheating. However, "loaded" dice have been around for years. These are dice which are weighted, or have rounded edges or other alterations resulting in one side or one set of numbers coming up more often than another.[3]

Playing with coins betting on the fall of heads or tails, can also be a fraud. Cheats modify their coins by chamfering the edges so that they fall on one side more often than the other.[4]

All told, fraud systems and devices are very common in gambling. Gambling with friends is hazardous enough, but gambling with strangers is a sucker's game, indeed.

NOTES

1. *Short Cons,* Scot Tinker, Eden Press, 1977, pp. 9-10.

2. *The Bunko Book,* Walter B. Gibson, 1976, Gambler's Book Club, pp. 50-58.

3. Ibid., pp. 41-49.

4. Ibid., p. 58.

HEALTH CARE FRAUD

The success of health care frauds provides a conspicuous exception to the widely-held belief that "you can't cheat an honest man." The victim is not seeking treatment out of greed, or in the hope of getting something for nothing.

This field is extraordinarily complicated, and we shall see that frauds are perpetrated by licensed medical men as well as "fly-by-night" types. We shall also see that in some instances fraud artists are protected by law, incredible as it might seem.

Let's start our survey with some obvious frauds. It's well known and widely accepted that a doctor must see his patient in person in order to examine him and prescribe proper treatment. Yet, in Tampa, Florida, a licensed physician was convicted of treating patients by mail order.[1] The physician involved had a degree in osteopathy, not an M.D., but osteopaths are recognized and licensed in most states, and their training is as comprehensive as that of M.D.s.

Another type of medical fraud is practicing medicine without a license. It is impossible to ascertain the number of bogus doctors in this country because detecting a fake is very difficult in practice. There have been a number of spectacular imposters who have played doctor, sometimes for years.

Typically, the way they do it is to assume the identify of a real doctor. While a fake diploma from a non-existent medical school may fool a patient, a hospital administrator will be more sophisticated and recognize it immediately as a fake. In the cases which have come to light, the imposter presented impeccable credentials in the name of a real graduate. It is standard practice to send for the transcripts of the records, and these did check out. In the cases in which the bogus doctors were exposed, it came about that another member of the staff had been to the same medical school at the same time, and did not remember the imposter. It is obvious that, with the large numbers of medical directories available, the employer did not do his homework. If a person presents himself as being "Dr. George Smith," it is not only possible to verify his medical school and licensing records, but it's easy to check the name in the Directory of Medical Specialists or the American Medical Association listing. It's also easy to check with the local medical association from the locale the applicant claims origin.

It is a difficult task for the patient to check out his physician. He does not have the time or investigative resources to do so, and usually does not even know how. There have been instances in which even a government agency has been slow to react. A bogus "Doctor" of psychology applied for, and got, a job as chief psychologist at the state prison of one of the smaller states. He held this position for almost a year before the administrators completed their investigation and found that his qualifications were false. **During this time, he expanded his horizons.** In collaboration with a former inmate of the prison, a man convicted of fraud and paroled after serving nineteen months, the bogus psychologist took to spending time at a local exclusive (high priced) resort, where he did his best to make the acquaintance of wealthy people. In one instance, he became acquainted with a very wealthy local auto dealer who was having problems with his marriage, and undertook to "counsel" him at the rate of fifty dollars an hour, which was a substantial fee at the time, 1970.[2] Meanwhile, the psychologist had defaulted on payments on a rented car, and stood off the agents who came to reclaim it by telling them they had no authority on state property, where he lived. **The prison provided its officers with living accommodations** on campus as it were, with security provided by the guard force.

This "psychologist" had the usual impressive credentials, including expensively printed diplomas. Few people realize that diploma blanks with decorative borders are stock items with printers, and that most printers will print anything the customer wants without question, except for obviously illegal counterfeiting of U.S. currency.[3]

Finally, the "psychologist's" bogus past caught up with him, and the prison authorities informed him that he could no longer continue in their employ. Strangely, they did not arrest or prosecute him, but merely gave him ten days to pack up his belongings and move out of the house which they had provided. He drifted to another state, where he had previously been charged with using the title "Doctor" without a license, and took up other scams to earn his living.

For many decades, the American Medical Association has acted to require strict licensing requirements for physicians, in an effort to drive out the quacks who get their diplomas from diploma mills or print them outright. They have been successful, in that many outright quacks have been put out of business, but it's important to note that there is also an element of self-interest at work. Often portrayed as the most powerful union in the nation, the AMA has been very protective of doctor's privileges. Recently, it took to the U.S. Supreme Court a case in which a local medical society was accused of price fixing, claiming that establishing prices for services rendered should be exempted from the law that applies to other businessmen. The Court decided against the AMA in this one.

The AMA takes very seriously any doctor who attempts to undercut the prices of his colleagues. In other fields, providing better service at lower cost is common practice, but not in medicine.

It's also worth noting that doctors often own stock in hospitals, which brings up the question of conflict of interest. Hospital costs have been in the headlines very much lately, with doctors claiming that hospitals are jacking up prices beyond all reason. Yet they continue to send their patients to hospitals without checking to determine which ones offer the lowest prices. They continue to admit patients to hospitals for procedures that require only office surgery or treatment in outpatient centers.

A good example is the doctors' attacks on the home birth movement. Doctors are almost unanimous in their contention that home birth involves risk if there are complications, and the home **birth practitioners point out that until the Twentieth Century, most babies were born at home, and in many parts of the world** still are. They say that it is possible to take care of high-risk pregnancies in a hospital, and have the rest delivered at home. Doctors, of course, see their income threatened by this, and oppose it bitterly, saying that only hospitalization can cope with the risks of pregnancy and birth, failing to point out that the United States, with its abundance of hospitals, does *not* have the lowest infant mortality rate in the world, which we would expect from this level of care. In one instance, a local hospital threatened to revoke the privileges of one doctor who delivered his patients' babies at home.

The AMA has had a running gunfight with alternate health care practitioners for decades, throwing them in with the quacks, and maintaining the position that nobody except a graduate of an AMA-approved medical school can be competent to care for patients. Chiropractors, for example, have been on the receiving end of an unrelenting attack, despite the fact that there are many people who have been helped by chiropratic.

Medical doctors claim a patient may suffer because he may have a serious illness that the chiropractor is not competent to diagnose and treat. There is another side to this coin. One man, for example, had been suffering from tension headaches resulting from stress on the job. His medical doctor had prescribed a tranquilizer, which turned out to be ineffective in coping with the headaches and left him with a groggy, dopey feeling that impaired his effectiveness on the job. Against his better judgement, because he had little faith in chiropractors, he consulted one. He had immediate relief from his headaches.[4]

The central fact about alternate health care is that the issues are not clear cut. First, established medicine is not completely aboveboard. Licensed physicians continue to prescribe unneeded treatments and unnecessary surgery to line their pockets.

Unnecessary operations are known in medical jargon as "renumer ectomies," and their occurance is so well known as not to require further discussion here.

Another unethical surgical practice is known as "ghost surgery," in which the surgeon who actually performs the operation is not the one whom the patient has been seeing, but a lower paid resident or intern. This enables the surgeon who subcontracts the work to handle a heavier caseload, collect full-size fees, and make a profit on each operation after paying the "ghost."

Thus we see that even licensed medical doctors are not all totally honest. Whether they are competent is another question, and an important one because the medical establishment claims that those who are not M.D.s are bad because they are not capable of treating patients.

Doctors make mistakes, some more than others. Yet, they are very reluctant to admit this. It is dirty linen which they do not air in public view. Most of us have had the experience of an illness which a doctor was not able to treat successfully, or have had relatives who were unsuccessfully treated by an M.D. We also see, in reading medical journals, wheedling phrases such as "the patient did not respond to therapy" or "...the patient's progress was disappointing..." which imply that it was the patient's and not the doctor's fault that he did not do well. Granted that there are uncertainties in medicine, when we get to how the doctor collects his fee we can see how differently he performs from other people who provide services. The doctor presents his bill whatever the outcome. We do not expect this from those in other occupations. We don't expect to pay a mechanic if he doesn't solve the problem with the car. Moreover, reputable mechanics warranty their work. If, after payment, the problem still exists or recurs, we return the car and expect satisfaction.

Non-performance by auto mechanics, plumbers, carpenters and electricians can result in complaints to the Better Business Bureau, and cases in small claims court. Non-performance is breach of contract. When a major corporation, for example, fails to perform properly the work it contracts with the Defense Department, the result is sometimes a lawsuit involving a substantial amount of money, as in the instance of National Semiconductor recently.[5]

Other parts of the medical establishment require a close look. The "ethical" drug companies have for years sold prescription and non-prescription drugs that were ineffective. Over the last few years, action by the Food and Drug Administration has forced the withdrawal of ineffective drugs, and one of the standards for new drugs is that they must do what they're supposed to do. The burden of proof is now on the drug company seeking to market the new drug, and it must submit to the FDA proof of effectiveness as well as proof of safety for use in humans.

The standards are still lax, and we find on the shelves many preparations with supposed medicinal value that actually do not work. The profusion of diet pills is a good example. None of these cause weight loss, and the leaflet that comes in the package usually provides a diet which the user must follow. It's clear that following the diet causes the weight reduction, not the ingredients of the pills.

Diet preparations are only part of the problem. There are innumerable others cleverly advertised to attract buyers without making claims that are in flagrant violation of the law. Baldness cures, complexion products, and others that fall into the category of cosmetics follow the same pattern.

They are all overpriced. Few buyers know the margin of profit involved. A preparation that contains petroleum jelly, lanolin, a weak concentration of a vitamin, and scent often sells for several dollars. It costs just a few cents to manufacture, and is usually a standard formula, not a "new beauty secret" as claimed.

It is still legal to produce and sell ineffective preparations, providing that the seller avoids infringing the weak laws governing them. There are many loopholes, and the largest companies employ staffs of lawyers who work to find and exploit these loopholes.

Turning to the outright illegal efforts which have been successfully prosecuted, we start with the case of two chiropractors who treated cancer, epilepsy, and other serious illnesses with a machine of their own invention. They also offered a diagnostic service by mail-order, at fifty bucks a throw. As part of its investigation, the California Department of Public Health had an agent send blood samples from a sheep, a pig, and a turkey to the "diagnostic laboratory." The diagnoses offered were chicken-pox and mumps.[6]

The field of cancer cures is very lucrative, with both real and bogus practitioners selling drugs that have proven ineffective. Often, they claim the medical establishment is conspiring to suppress their discoveries because a real cancer cure would mean a loss of income for doctors. This has a core of truth, and people who have had disappointing experiences with greedy doctors find it easier to accept.

The bedside manners of "real" M.D.s do not build confidence. Many of them are arrogant and brusque, and it is general practice for them to keep patients waiting for their appointments and then process them in a manner like that of a supermarket checkout.[7] **By contrast, the bogus drug sellers and other fake practitioners** have kindly, sympathetic approaches. They are masters at winning people over. They are con men. This is the real reason for their continuing successes.

A formerly licensed physician distributed "liefcort," a valueless drug, by mail-order.[8] "Krebiozen" is another, more widely publicized drug which has turned out to be worthless but which has earned large sums for its distributors.[9] A recent effort was the promotion of "Laetrile", a supposed cure for cancer. While many people claim to have been helped by Laetrile, it has been banned in the United States.[10] It is now being offered to cancer sufferers in Mexican border towns, where Americans come for treatments.[11]

As we've seen, one reason that people choose to try some of the bogus artists is their experiences with M.D.s have been unpleasant. Another is that conventional medical treatment has failed. Conventional medicine has failed to find a cure for arthritis, a chronic illness which, although not usually fatal, is so painful in some cases that the patient might well wish it were. A cancer patient who has spent much money on conventional doctors may feel that, with his life at stake, he'll try anything, as he has nothing to lose. While the quack may truly be incompetent, licensed physicians also misdiagnose cases and prescribe the wrong treatment.[12] To the patient who is desperate, any hope is worth following up and grasping.

Some of the medical frauds are outlandish. They involve bizarre machines and procedures, and promise "miracle" cures. One scam had the victims sitting in worked-out uranium mines where the radioactivity had supposed curative powers.[13] Another sold copper bracelets as cures for arthritis. Some are in the weight-reducing business.

On the fringes of health care are many others, such as naturopaths, homeopaths, hypnotists, and various "counselors." It would be wrong to label all of these quacks, as the scientific foundation proving or disproving the value of their work is by no means clear. There are no clear-cut rules of thumb to distinguish the quack from the legitimate practitioner.

If we judge a con man by his smooth and considerate manner, we must admit there are doctors who show much consideration for their patients.

If we look for bizarre equipment that works according to arcane principles, we'll find it hard to distinguish a CAT scanner from an orgone box without specialized and technical knowledge.

If we judge by results, it will be difficult to decide if successful or unsuccessful cases are good indices of the worth of a treatment. While the surgeons who performed heart transplants developed international reputations, most of their patients died. The widely-publicized artificial heart has not been an outstanding success, to say the least. Doctors still can't cure colds. This confusing picture points up how truly difficult it is to spot a "quack."

What complicates the picture even more is that some of these disapproved cures *work*. Hypnotists, for example, do get results in some cases, and in crime investigation hypnotism is slowly gaining acceptance as a means of clarifying a witness's hazy memory.[14] Hypnotists are able to help in various psychological disorders, and implant posthypnotic suggestions that help people with weight and smoking problems. However, failure or success depends a lot on the skill of the individual hypnotists, and there is no reliable way to predict results, despite the claims of hypnotists who seek to promote themselves.

The operators who run weight loss clinics and anti-smoking clinics are in a similar position. While there is no doubt that reducing excess weight and stopping smoking are beneficial, how to do it best is the controversy. Despite the proliferation of novel ideas, doctors, dieticians, and many layman understand that the only way to lose weight is to take in fewer calories than are burned. The only method of effective, long-term weight loss is for the person to modify his eating so that he eats consistently just enough to counterbalance his calorie burn. Less, and he'll lose weight. More, and he'll gain weight.

Similarly, the only way to stop smoking is to stop. Very many people have tried to taper off without success, and others who try to stop but backslide by mooching an occasional cigarette soon provoke the comment, "You haven't stopped smoking, you've just stopped buying."

Such clinics vary in effectiveness. Obviously, not everyone will succeed, as motivation is very important. The key to whether these clinics are frauds or not is in the motivation of the operator, and this is very hard to ascertain. We can't judge totally by results for, as we have seen, intense efforts by sincere and well-motivated people can fail, as in the case of the artificial heart.

"Counselors" are special cases. The term is often a simple device to practice clinical psychology while avoiding prosecution. Many states require that anyone who practices as a psychologist be licensed, and to obtain a license the applicant must have passed a certain course of study, and fulfilled other requirements such as practical experience under the supervision of a licensed psychologist.

Mental healing, if we can call it that, is not a science. Unlike the physical sciences, there are no tangible objects to measure, and there is often disagreement as to what doctrine or treatment is correct. Physicians who embark on mental healing are called psychiatrists, unlike psychologists who have extensive psychological training but no medical degree.

Those who don't have training in one field or another, or insufficient training to call themselves doctors or psychologists can, in many states, call themselves "counselors."

Counselors come in many shapes, sizes, and degrees of competence. Some may be actual psychologists, complete with Ph.D.s. Others are graduates of obscure colleges, or even diploma mills. In some areas, they have no qualifications at all.

Treatment of mental problems is at best uncertain. The "legitimate" psychiatrists and psychologists disagree about the structure of the mind, the extent to which physical factors affect the mind, and ways to change behavior and suppress symptoms of mental disorder and to help the patient adjust to his situation. The psychiatrist looks down upon the psychologists, and the psychologists themselves follow different "schools" of thought.

Certain charismatic and well-known practitioners have established "schools," or followings, which adhere to their theories and usually are named after them, such as Freud, Jung, Horney, Sullivan and White. The various "complexes" which they blame for mental problems have often turned out to be normal emotional development or even nonexistent except in the analyst's mind. In conventional psychiatry, the emphasis has been on treating mental problems with physical methods, such as shock treatment, psychosurgery, and drugs, most of which have proven to have side effects which are more severe than the disorder.

Often, treatment of an emotional problem, from psychosis to relatively modest marital problems, has consisted mainly of "psychotherapy," in which the practitioner attempts to establish rapport, or confidence, with the patient, and persuade him to change his way of thinking and his behavior. This process bears a remarkable resemblance to both salesmanship and to religious experience, in which the main ingredient is faith.

Taking up the question of how much harm is done by "counselors" who don't have "legitimate" credentials, we must consider that many people with emotional problems derive no benefit from "legitimate" practitioners. Emotional problems, being intangible, are more difficult to diagnose and treat. There is no tumor to cut out, no fever to bring down.

Some psychosomatic illnesses can lead a patient to unnecessary treatment and even harm at the hands of a "real" doctor, if he doesn't recognize the cause. Psychosomatic symptoms, although mainly in the patient's mind, are no less real than physical ones and often doctors apply physical measures to cure them. One category, called "polysurgery" leads the patient to consult surgeons in attempts to have surgery performed.[15] In such instances, conventional and reputable surgeons perform multiple unneeded operations upon these patients, with the usual risks of side effects that apply to all surgery.

In conventional medical practice, a new word has sprung up. "Iatrogenic" means symptoms and disorders caused by the doctor's treatment. A drug side-effect is iatrogenic. Complications of surgery are iatrogenic, all of which confuse the picture further.

The patient with a psychosomatic disorder, who consults a quack who is not permitted or likely to attempt surgery, at least saves himself the risk of complications. The one with an imaginary illness who consults a faith healer may even be "cured" of his disorder, without risky medical treatment.

This brings us to the question of faith and religious healers. Most of us have seen various religious figures who claim to heal the sick, and some of us have seen those who do this on television. There is cause to believe many of the symptoms are psychogenic. However, the imaginary paralysis or pain is no less real than one with a physical cause, as we've seen, and a psychological "cure" can be just as real as a physical one.

Religious healers comprise a gray area in our society and in our law. It is almost impossible to prosecute them, as they enjoy the protection of the First Amendment of our Constitution. In instances where money changes hands, or the practitioner operates a well-known fraud, prosecution is possible.[16] There are well-known bunco schemes based upon fraudulent religious practice. However, many religious practitioners are sincere, and whether their healing is valid is often hard to either establish or disprove.

Another area protected by the First Amendment is health care books. Each year brings its crop of diet books, and volumes on foot reflexology, iridology, and other forms of alternate health care. Each year those who have bought one or the other diet book and failed to lose weight buy a new one, hoping that the latest "system" will help them lose weight.

This is a lucrative field, because of the freedom to publish anything without either censorship or the obligation to check the material for validity. Thus, anyone can write anything he wants, without fear of accusations of charlatanism. It is perfectly legal, and often the only concession to the law is a disclaimer to the effect that the book is not intended as medical advice, but for informational purposes only.

Another very lucrative field is health food. The very real, and widely publicized, instances of large food producing companies using additives which are carcinogenic or which have other harmful effects has been a windfall for small hucksters who have touted their products as "natural." A pound of unrefined sugar, for example, sells for many times the price of the refined product, despite the less complicated processing. Sea salt commands a higher price, bought by people who believe that in using it they will get more essential elements than they do from refined salt (true), but ignoring the fact that our oceans are now polluted and they'll get their share of that, too.

All told, the field of health care can bring wealth to those adept in exploiting it. Unscrupulous frauds are not confined to the fly-by-nighters, but are used by even the "legitimate" practitioners, which makes it that much harder for the consumer to protect himself.

NOTES

1. *Classic Mail Frauds,* Scot Tinker, Eden Press, 1977, p. 32.

2. Personal knowledge of author. At the time, the author, who interviewed this "Doctor of Psychology" for a newspaper, visited his home and became well-acquainted with him. Although some of the statements this bogus psychologist made did not ring true, at the time the author accepted him as genuine because the state department of corrections had.

3. Personal knowledge of author, who works in the printing trades. Anyone can have business cards, letterheads, and other materials printed without question, and can later use them to convince a victim that he is the head of a corporation, a doctor, etc. While this may seem irregular, it's important to note that printers are not legally or morally obligated to check out the

provenance of each customer and each job they accept, and that most of them are legitimate, in the end.

4. Personal acquaintance of author.

5. United Press, March 7, 1984. National Semiconductor had failed to perform the required "burn-in" tests on chips sold to the Defense Department, tests which would eliminate defective chips. The criminal indictment resulted in almost two million dollars' worth of penalties.

6. *Fraud Investigation,* Glick and Newsom, 1974, Charles C. Thomas, Publisher, pp. 234-5.

7. Personal experiences of author, who has been kept waiting in doctor's waiting rooms for appointments. In one instance, the doctor was over an hour late, and upon arrival laughingly said to the author, "Well, you don't have anything else to do today, anyway."

8. *Fraud Investigation,* p. 252.

9. Ibid, p. 252.

10. Ibid, p. 252.

11. Personal knowledge of author. An acquaintance, a 23-year old man with testicular cancer, went to Mexico to obtain Laetrile treatments. Some months afterwards, he died of cancer, which had spread through his body.

12. The author's father, who died of lung cancer, was first diagnosed as having pleurisy, and told to take a rest cure at a resort town. Two years later, another M.D. diagnosed his illness as cancer, too late to save his life. The original physician collected his bill nevertheless.

13. *A Compendium of Bunk or How to Spot a Con Artist,* Carey and Sherman, Charles C. Thomas, 1976, p. 197.

14. *Law and Order,* periodical, February 1984, pp. 52-4.

15. *Man Against Himself,* Karl Meninger, M.D., Harcourt, Brace and Co., New York, 1938. pp. 259-277. The phenomenon of patients visiting doctors and presenting imaginary illnesses is well-known in the medical profession, and these people are windfalls for "knife-happy" surgeons. Medical publications devote very little

space to the question of how many such people are victimized by unscrupulous doctors. It's easier to ignore the problem, or to pretend it does not exist. In any case, "whistle-blowers" are ostracized by doctors, as they are in other fields.

16. *Fraud Investigation*, pp. 253-255.

SPECIAL NOTE ON SOURCES:

In all the literature examined to gather background material for this chapter, there was no mention of the *placebo effect*, which often operates in obtaining "cures." The placebo effect is well-known to doctors, and even more to researchers. A patient will sometimes get well even through the administration of an inert substance. For some, a sugar pill or an injection of sterile water will cause remission of their symptoms.

Medical researchers use this in checking out new drugs. A group of patients used for the test is divided in two, with one half getting the new drug and the other half the placebo. Neither group knows whether the "drug" it gets is the placebo or the real thing. It often happens that the group getting the placebo has a certain number of successes, and the measure of the new drug's effectiveness is the difference in success rates between the group getting the actual drug and that of the control group, which gets the placebo.

There are several possible reasons for the placebo effect:

1. The body heals itself in many instances. A headache will eventually disappear, pill or no pill.

2. Suggestion is a very powerful mechanism. The healer, by telling the patient that his treatment will help him, uses suggestion. This works better with some people than with others.

3. Faith and other psychological factors. We could say that "faith" is another term for "suggestion," but there are some as yet unexplored and unproven psychological effects involved in cures. These intangible factors explain partly why a certain patient will fare better with one doctor than with another, or with an alternative practitioner better than with a conventional M.D. It is not always fraud, but the psychological mechanisms in both are very similar.

INCOME OPPORTUNITY
AND JOB OFFER FRAUDS

Each day, there are advertisements that begin with "Make Money at Home." Generally, these are ripoffs, but they come in so many varieties they're worth a close look.

The simplest type is the "training school" ad. There are legitimate training schools, and most of these offer classroom instruction in technical subjects such as electronics and air conditioning repair, their only fault being that they tend to exaggerate the demand for these skills in the job market and quote somewhat high rates of pay for those with the skills they teach. This is a good example of where legitimate business overlaps fraud.

Correspondence schools are another matter. Some are accredited institutions, and even have various seals of approval, such as those given out by the Veteran's Administration. Others are sleazy operations that offer the student only the opportunity to give away his money. Among the worst are those that have courses in "detective" training. Whoever sends away for the "free information" gets a brochure that promises him substantial income in a lucrative and growing field. Sometimes, he is further enticed by the promise of "free" equipment supplied with the course. Among the "free" items offered by some are small personal computers and "detective" badges. In reality, the student pays for everything, although there may not be itemization of each item.

Many of these courses offer time payments, sometimes carrying the contract themselves, sometimes passing on the contract to a finance company for a commission.

For anyone considering a correspondence course, it's a smart move to contact potential employers in the field and ask whether they would hire someone who is a graduate of that course, and what the pay would be.

Some advertisements are worded so vaguely that it is very unclear just what the money-making scheme is. Typically, these are full-page ads, filled with blurbs calculated to build anticipation and induce the reader to send in his ten or twenty dollars without knowing exactly how he'll become rich. Often, these ads will carry a photograph of the operator standing next to a Cadillac, Jaguar, or Rolls-Royce which he claims to own, and promise that those who answer the ad will soon enjoy the same high economic status.

Some earn-money-at-home schemes involve buying a kit of tools and materials, or a machine, to produce goods that the company will allegedly buy back. The cost to the victim can run from a few dollars to many hundreds, and he has to sign an agreement to buy all of his material from the company.

The problem arises when the victim has finished his first lot and sends it to the buyer. Invariably, the buyer returns it, claiming the workmanship is not up to the company's quality standards.[1]

A variant of this tactic is to offer materials to make a product which the company claims the victim will have no difficulty in selling to his friends and neighbors or door-to-door. The product is not as easy to sell as the company claims.

Employment agencies offer great opportunities for fraud of one sort or another. Although almost every locale in the country has a branch of the state employment service, and almost every newspaper carries legitimate employment ads, there are still "private" employment agencies that offer jobs to applicants. Some of these agencies are legitimate, but others are not.

Theoretically, an employment agency works for the jobseeker, because it collects the fee from him. Most often, the applicant is required to sign a contract in which he agrees to pay a percentage of his first year's salary, or one month's wages, for the job referral. Sometimes, it's hard to see what he gets for this.

One marginal operation, operating in a state in which there was a constant supply of newcomers, earned fees by simply referring the applicant to the telephone company's employment office, after a cursory interview. The operator did not even disturb himself by trying to match the applicant to the job. Most referrals did not find employment at the phone company, but those who did were legally required to pay the agency a substantial fee.

In theory, the agency operator contacts employers in an effort to find a job to suit the applicant. As we've seen, some operators don't work very hard at this. Others have schemes in which they're in collusion with some local employers with flexible ethics. They give the employer a kickback taken from the fee that the applicant pays them.

Sometimes, the side-effects of this practice can be very pernicious. The foreman or manager of a company that uses mainly unskilled labor, for example, knows that he'll get a kickback for each person whom he hires from a particular agency. This gives him an incentive to fire or lay off employees and hire new ones, of course accepting referrals from the agency which pays kickbacks. This practice does not work well with skilled labor, as employee turnover causes problems in that new employees need a period of "breaking in" to their complex jobs.

In major cities, there are resume writing services that offer a reasonably professional product for the fee. However, even this "service" is open to exploitation by the con artist. The scheme is very much the same as the bogus employment agency, so we'll look at them in parallel.

The operator rents an office and places his advertisements offering jobs. He tells the applicants that he'll refer them, or send out their resumes, explaining that he will not collect a fee until the applicant is in his new job.

After a few days, the operator notifies the applicant that he has an appointment with the personnel manager of a large corporation that will be opening up a facility in his city. The personnel manager will be conducting interviews in his hotel room, and the applicant has a specific appointment. The applicant arrives at the appointed time for the interview. The "personnel manager" is a confederate who sizes him up for the final stage of the scheme.

He invites those who seem gullible enough for a final interview in a couple of weeks' time. This gives the operators time enough to line up more victims. When the applicant shows up for the final interview, the "personnel manager" tells him that he thinks that he's very suitable for the job, but that he'll hire him in spite of his having been referred by the resume writing service or employment agency. He adds that the company has had some negative experience with employees not paying their fees and having their wages garnished. He states that those who did had been summarily fired, as the company did not want to be annoyed by acting as a collection agency for a third party. The applicant would have to pay off his fee and present a receipt the next day to enable the "personnel manager" to go through with the final stage of hiring him.

At this point, the applicants who can scrape up the money pay the fee to the operator. After collecting the fees, the swindlers leave town.[2]

Pyramid sales are another common scam. While there are legitimate dealerships, such as those run by Avon and Fuller Brush, there are those run by fast operators who are only selling dreams to the unwary.

Generally, the scheme is for each applicant to buy a certain volume of the company's products, and set himself up as a "distributor." The fraud artist tells him the products are easy to sell, and the applicant can increase his profits by recruiting "dealers," each dealer buying a certain amount of inventory.

There is usually a lot of hype involved in these schemes. Typically, the operator holds meetings attended by many candidates for dealerships and distributorships. There are films portraying the opulent lifestyles enjoyed by those who have allegedly succeeded in this plan, and enthusiastic statements by shills who claim that they were poverty-stricken until they joined the plan and brought themselves into riches.[3]

These are called "pyramid" schemes because the success of each level of dealers and distributors depends on winning new victims and selling inventory to them. Very little filters out to the general public, and the products involved are cosmetics, motor products, and other non-perishable goods. The plan, if diagrammed, would look exactly like that of a chain letter.[4]

Another type of fraud that promises its victims substantial income is the invention development scheme. The operator places advertisements that begin with the word INVENTORS, and goes on to state that the operator's firm specializes in evaluating and promoting new inventions, and assisting the inventor in getting it patented. There are some people who think they've devised a new invention, and if they reply to one of these ads, they'll find the company will tell them their idea has unusual merit, and because of this, the normal fee would be reduced. They find out that they have to pay several hundred dollars for processing the paperwork, and sometimes find the company asks them for more money to cover the expenses incurred while promoting the idea to manufacturers. There may or may not be an application for a patent. Most people are not aware that there is no requirement by the U.S. Patent Office that the invention actually work, and there are many thousands of ideas patented that have no value whatsoever.

Whatever the details of the scheme, the basic mechanism is to ask the inventor for more payment from time to time, allegedly to use in promotion of his invention. Although there have been some convictions in this scheme, we still see this swindle advertised today.[5]

There are a lot of people in this country who fancy themselves to be writers, and there is a segment of business that thrives upon these people and their dreams of glory. All of them employ deception to some extent.

While there are legitimate literary agents, and some of the best-known writers work through agents because agents know the market for their writings and can negotiate the best contracts for them, there are also many unknown writers who fall victim to either bogus literary agents or to legitimate agencies whose owners take the opportunity to pick up some extra money on the side.

The operators advertise for writers to send them their manuscripts. Typically, there is a reading fee of from fifty to one hundred dollars. In return for this fee, the agents deliver an evaluation of the work, and if it's good enough to sell, will try to do so.

The dishonest operators will not give honest evaluations, as that would involve telling some of their clients they had no talent and would be better off spending their time doing something else. Each manuscript, whatever the quality, as long as it is accompanied by the required fee, gets the same answer. The writer "shows promise" but the manuscript is "a little rough" and should be revised and resubmitted, accompanied by another fee, for re-evaluation. If the writer cares to submit other manuscripts, the operator will be happy to evaluate them, too, for a fee.

Sometimes the operator can milk an aspiring writer for these modest sums for an almost unbelievable time. Each manuscript that comes to him is an opportunity to generate repeat business, if he can persuade the writer it's worthwhile to revise it and resubmit it.

Closely allied to these bogus literary schemes are the subsidy publishers, sometimes derisively called "the vanity press." They play on the well-known fact that some people will pay substantial sums to see their names in print, and be able to claim they are published authors.

Some of the subsidy publishers are quite upfront about explaining the arrangement, that the author pays the costs of editing, typesetting, paste-up and printing, and the publisher and the author will split the proceeds of the sales in an agreed percentage. Others are not so forthright. They con the authors, complimenting them lavishly on the quality and significance of their work, and suggesting it's likely to be a runaway bestseller. First, however, there are certain formalities, certain expenses....

Among the correspondence courses advertised are artist's and writer's schools. As with other such enterprises, some are legitimate, and some aren't. Whatever the case, the format is the same. The applicant responds to an advertisement for a "free"aptitude test, which the staff of the school will evaluate. Theoretically, if he shows promise, he'll receive encouragement to sign up for the school's course. In practice, the evaluation the victim gets back tells him he shows great promise, and is sure to be a success if he takes the course and polishes his skill, under the watchful eyes of the school's skilled instructors.[6] The course runs for many months, is expensive, and the victim can pay as he goes.

Some of the schools carry their own contracts, and allow the student to pay for each lesson as he gets it. The ones run by the most flagrant of the fly-by-nights have the victim sign a credit contract with a finance company, collect the money, and leave town suddenly.

One of the more recent frauds involves employment ads seeking "karate instructors." When the victim applies for the job, he hears, quite logically, that he must be qualified in order to be able to teach. The operator tells him that he needs more training, obtainable at his school, before he can qualify for the job. If the victim bites, he signs up for a course without any guarantee that at the end he'll be "qualified" for the job. This is a device used by operators of store-front self-defense schools to stimulate business, and is a good example of how legitimate businesses can overlap into fraudulent practices.

NOTES

1. *Fraud Investigation*, Glick and Newsom, Charles C. Thomas, 1974, pp. 220-222.

2. *Short Cons,* Scot Tinker, Eden Press, 1977, p. 32.

3. Personal knowledge of author, who attended one of these meetings while reporting for a newspaper. The atmosphere was contrived, with much shouting by shills planted in the audience, and outlandish promises of how the "dealers" could, with minimal investments, go from rags to riches in an astonishingly short time. The operator later went to prison.

4. *Big Time Operator's Manual,* Scot Tinker, 1977, Eden Press, pp. 42-43.

5. *Classic Mail Frauds,* Scot Tinker, Eden Press, 1977, p. 23.

6. Personal experience of author, who can't draw a straight line without a ruler. He sent in an "artist's aptitude test" completed in the most incompetent way possible, and got back a glowing letter telling him that he "showed great promise," that his latent skill and esthetic perceptions needed to be "developed," and that the school offered a course that would do this, at a one-time-only price that was a substantial discount from the regular price.

INSURANCE

During the Great Depression, insurance companies were the only class of American business that made money consistently. Not only did they survive, but they thrived. Today, insurance companies own many other companies, as they have invested the billions they've collected in premiums, while paying out very little to beneficiaries.

Insurance is a good example of a type of business (auto dealerships and medicine are two others) that started out for a worthwhile purpose and gradually evolved into what amounts to legalized fraud. The basis for the fraud is misrepresentation of the contract and its benefits to the client. Typically, the sales pitch will tell how the plan will give the insured financial protection so he may feel secure. Some pitches, especially the commercials on TV, feature a celebrity who exclaims to the listeners that "you cannot be turned down or cancelled," and the premiums are low and affordable. The reality is quite different, as the buyer will find out when he reads the fine print.

A long-standing joke about insurance is that the company will pay off only if the insured is involved in an airplane crash which takes place at midnight in a subway tunnel on the 29th of February, leap year. The fine print contains so many exceptions and exclusions that often the client does not get the benefits he thinks he will be getting.[1]

There is a saying: "read the fine print," which applies to any contract, but especially insurance contracts. This bears directly on the main point: insurance contracts have a lot of fine print, and the reason for this is to make it difficult for the client to understand what he's getting and more importantly, what he's *not* getting. It's wrong to think insurance companies have their contracts in fine print to save on the cost of paper and printing. With their billions of dollars in assets, insurance companies need not worry about that. The real reason is to make the contracts hard to read, especially for elderly people with failing eyesight. The wording of the contract is another story.

Typically, insurance contracts proliferate multisyllabic terminology, including many redundant technicalities in a maze of repetitive dependent clauses, and these polysyllabic redundancies impede, rather than facilitate, comprehension for the person who lacks the requisite training and familiarity. Like this paragraph, they are hard to read.

This is not a coincidence. Insurance companies design them to be hard to read, to make it almost impossible for the client to understand what he is getting and what he's been led to believe he's getting are not the same. Only a lawyer can understand them. Even the insurance salesman often doesn't. He's been instructed in how to pitch the policy to the customer, and how to answer questions. He doesn't have to worry about the fine print, because the sales department does not process claims. When the client makes a claim, he'll find the claims department is far less friendly than the salesman.

NOTES

1. *A Compendium of Bunk,* Carey and Sherman, Charles C. Thomas, 1976, pp. 134-135.

INTENTIONAL ACCIDENTS

Homeowners and small businessmen may often worry about bad checks, but there are more dramatic swindles to which they are vulnerable. One of them is the intentional accident artist, or "flop" artist. There are innumerable instances of "bone breakers" who "accidentally" throw themselves in front of automobiles and collect for their injuries. One unpleasant fact which confuses the issue is that some injuries, while real, are intangible, as in whiplash of the neck. It is a well-documented fact that whiplash can cause lingering symptoms, such as pain and dizziness, but it's also true that these symptoms cannot be detected, measured, or verified by any tests. The doctor, the lawyer, and the insurance company have only the sufferer's word. There are many compliant doctors and lawyers who help to magnify any symptom, legitimate or not, that the victim suffers in order to extract as large a settlement as possible. In one instance, a firm of lawyers advertises on television that one of the partners, besides being a lawyer, also has a medical degree.

Considering outright frauds, we come to the "rusty nail" swindle. The fraud artist orders a meal in a restaurant and while eating, makes a cut inside his mouth with a razor blade. He yells, and spits out a rusty staple or nail. Claiming that the offending item was in the food, he sues, or threatens to sue. As many such suits are settled out of court, the fraud artist often finds it easy and quick to extract money from the scheme.[1]

A variant on this personal-injury theme is the "spilled wax" swindle. The con-man, playing the role of customer in a supermarket or other retail outlet, uncaps a bottle of liquid wax while unobserved and spills some on the floor. The substance need not be wax, as there are many items and compounds that can make a floor slippery, such as ice, a banana peel, etc.

When another customer appears in the aisle, the con man "takes a fall," crashing to the floor and feigning dazedness. Of course, the other customer will usually try to help him, having been a witness to the incident, and the store manager will rush to the scene. The victim takes a trip to a hospital, complaining of pain in the head and neck. This sets the scene for a lawsuit, the threat of a lawsuit, or a quick settlement out of court.[2]

A businessman or his insurance carrier, while they may be suspicious, often have no defense against this practice. Insurance companies, as a means of protecting themselves against such scams, keep detailed records of claims against them, in the hope of establishing that the complainant has a record of prior claims, which would count heavily in court if the insurance company can show a pattern. This technique does not always work, as many con artists use false identities in these games.[3]

NOTES

1. *Professional Con Games, Schemes, and Frauds*, 1979, Carl Dorski, Roadrunner Publications, PO Box 572, Keego Harbor, MI 48033, p. 19.

2. Ibid. p. 20.

3. *The Paper Trip, I and II*, Eden Press.

INTERNATIONAL FRAUDS

Crime, like business, does not stop at a nation's border. For both legal and tactical reasons, it often pays for a criminal to operate in two or more countries. An act that calls for a heavy sentence in one country involves a lesser penalty in another. It may not even be illegal. For example, a quirk in the counterfeiting laws of most countries makes it illegal to counterfeit only that particular country's currency, but says nothing about another's.

Other countries make good hosts, perhaps because they permit secret bank accounts, or have no extradition treaties. Switzerland and Brazil are traditional examples of this.

The most practical reason for operating across national lines, especially for the con man, is he can depend on the usual lack of cooperation and coordination between police forces to work in his favor. There are jurisdictional limits. There are language barriers.

Let's look at a real-life example to see how this works:

Paris, France, in 1969 was a good place for an American tourist speaking French. The food was good, and prices had not yet risen out of sight. An American couple getting off a tourist river boat was approached by a young lady:

"Pardon me, but you look like you're from the States."

"Yes we are."

"Well, we're having a little get-together for Americans tonight at the ——— Hotel. We'll have a buffet supper and some films. Would you and your wife like to come?"

That was the approach, delivered by an American girl studying in Paris and picking up some extra money by greeting marks and "steering" them to the main operation. Possibly she had no knowledge of anything beyond her very limited part in the scam.

When the couple showed up at the hotel, they found a dining room set up with a buffet table at one end. They gathered their meal together, sat down, and soon the salesman assigned to their table joined them. During and after the meal, the hosts showed films of a "vacationland paradise" in Florida, and the chief salesman explained that the assembled guests were getting a once-in-a-lifetime opportunity to invest and get rich.

In front of each place at the table was a small stack of papers. On top was a brochure, in color, telling of the land offer. At the bottom of the stack was a legal document issued by the Florida Land Commission, with some warnings on the top page. The warnings stated clearly that it was advisable to inspect personally any land offered, as it might be under water or deep in a swamp. When the husband lifted the other papers by a corner to peek at this bottom document, the salesman firmly slammed his palm down on the stack.

The rest of the evening was a typical "high-pressure" sales effort. One couple bought a parcel of land, early on, and the master of ceremonies loudly announced that "Parcel 101" was going out of circulation, and no longer available for sale. He had the buyers stand up and take a bow, and announce their reasons for buying. The M.C. visited each table, to oversee the proceedings. As the session drew on, the crowd began to thin out, most of the people not following the example set by the shills early on.

Among the last to leave were the couple we've been following. Fascinated by the affair, they stayed to hear it all, carefully refraining from signing anything. They earned the M.C.'s personal attention, and perhaps personal wrath, when he stopped at their table to inquire why they hadn't bought this tremendous offer. He turned offensive when he stated: "There are only two reasons why you haven't bought. Either you don't have the money or you don't trust me."

Instead of embarrassing the couple into signing, this challenge offered them a quick out. They simply pleaded poverty, telling the M.C. they'd saved for five years to come to Europe and only had their tickets and a few traveler's checks to their name. It was an outrageous lie, but no worse than the lies they'd been hearing all evening. They got up and left.[1]

Now let's examine closely what might have happened if they had signed, paid a deposit, and found they had been conned.

1. To whom would they have complained? The Paris Police? That depends on when they found out they'd been taken. The

property was in Florida, and neither husband nor wife had ever been to Florida. If they happened to go, and found their "recreational property" under water, and complained to the local sheriff, they'd surely be told the fraud was not committed in Florida, and they should complain to the police where it was.

2. Traveling around to investigate and make a complaint would be costly. Who could afford it? Who'd be able to take the time off from work?

3. Who can or will prosecute? Prosecution, difficult as it is, does happen when a fraud takes place in a local area, but an international affair such as this one creates a nightmare. A fraud, perpetrated by Americans only on other Americans who will not be long enough in Paris either to complain to the police or to testify if a prosecution should result, is an almost perfect bunco operation. It is patently illegal, but under whose law? The difficulties of following through with a prosecution are almost insurmountable.

NOTES

1. Personal experience of the author.

MONEY SWINDLES

There are several swindles that involve cash directly, and which fraud artists use on both ordinary citizens and small businessmen. Some are crude and simple, and others are so ingenious it is almost impossible to provide an adequate defense.

One of the oldest ones is check kiting. This term refers to establishing a checking account with a small balance, then drawing a check to establish another in another bank. The amount is larger than the funds in the first account, and the con man covers that check with one drawn on the second account. He then covers the one in the second account with an even larger one which he draws on the first account.[1]

This is the plan for simple check kiting, but there are more elaborate schemes, involving many accounts and a system of rotation to cover all of the bogus checks. In the complicated systems, it's critical to keep detailed records, and timing is extremely important to keep the different checks floating between the banks without running into each other.

One question that inevitably comes up when a class in elementary economics discusses kiting is: "Why is check kiting illegal, if all the checks are covered?" The reason is that, although the game may go on for months, the last check will not be covered. The amounts in the accounts may be fabulous, but they exist only on paper, and there is no "real" money to cover them.

Kiting is an old fraud, and does not work well anymore, for several reasons:

1. Today, it's common practice for banks to delay crediting an account with the amount of a deposit involving a check until the check clears. This is not a perfect defense, as with the elaborate systems a check can clear and be credited, but it stops the simple systems.

2. Bank employees all know what kiting is, and they're alert to the possibility of a checking account's being established for kiting. Kiting checks presents a pattern of deposits and withdrawal by check, with a deposit being followed by a check drawn for a larger

amount, followed by a deposit for an even larger amount, etc. The computers that post checks and deposits to the individual accounts are programmed to "flag" accounts that show a pattern that suggests kiting.

3. Electronic banking cuts the time needed for a check to clear drastically, and it is no longer possible for a check to float between accounts for weeks. The decline in the speed and efficiency of the U.S. Postal Service also works against check kiters if they bank by mail.

The phoney loan agency is another money swindle. A person who applies for a loan meets a sympathetic gentleman who assures him his *bona fides* appear good, and there should be no problem in securing the loan. However, the formalities include a background check, involving some expenses, and the prospective borrower must put up the front money for this. If the victim bites and passes over the money, he'll have a wait of several days or weeks before he gets a sympathetic letter informing him that, on the basis of the information developed in the background check, the request for the loan must be denied.[2]

There are several variations possible on this theme. This swindle is an easy one to work by mail, as all of the transactions can take place on paper, instead of with a face-to-face meeting. As the amounts involved can't be very large, the swindler must be able to continue operations in order to make substantial amounts from this scheme, and the critical part of the swindle is the "block," the device to keep the victim quiet while the swindler carries on.

The "block" is the loan application, which contains the statement that the fee required for background investigation is not refundable. Unless the victim is very perceptive, or very suspicious, he will not complain to the police, thinking that this legal document is legitimate.

Bad checks plague businessmen, and most retailers have established procedures by which the customer who offers a check must prove his identity, or present a check guarantee card that is valid only up to a certain amount. In cases of large checks, the businessman will check with the bank by telephone to verify there

95

is enough deposited in the account to cover the check. The clever swindler has an almost fool-proof way around this precaution. He opens a checking account at the bank, issues a few checks, then returns to the bank to report that he lost his checkbook or had it stolen, and requests that the bank close the account and start a new one. He makes a substantial deposit into the new account, enough to cover the amount of any purchase he plans with his scheme. When he gets the printed checks, they'll have his name, address, and phone number on them, with only the magnetically imprinted account number being different. However, the first digits of the two account numbers, identifying the bank and branch office, will match, as they'll have come from the same branch.

Working the swindle, the fraud artist makes an expensive purchase at a store during banking hours, the amount involved being so large that the store employee feels compelled to verify the validity of the check with the bank. The check which the con man hands over is drawn on the legitimate account. The telephone check establishes the validity of the account, and when the clerk returns with the check the con man decides on a different purchase and tears up the check, writing a new one from the check book belonging to the closed account. If he is especially nervy, he may write a check for more than the amount of the purchase, asking for the difference in cash, as long as the total does not exceed the amount that the clerk or manager had verified with the bank. Retailers almost never notice this switch.[3]

Another swindle, somewhat riskier but often pulled on retailers, is the Secret Service Agent Swindle. To carry this out, the swindler obtains a U.S. Secret Service letterhead. This is easy to do, requiring only a letter to the Secret Service on an unrelated matter. On a separate sheet of paper, the swindler types a circular pertaining to a new issue of counterfeit $100 bills that have come into circulation, and tapes this circular to the legitimate letter which he's received from the Secret Service. He photocopies the letter, placing a hundred dollar bill with the serial number enumerated in the letter at the bottom of the copy, below the signature of the genuine Secret Service Agent who signed.

The con man's partner, using this perfectly legitimate hundred-dollar bill, makes a purchase from a retailer. Later, before the retailer makes a cash deposit at his bank, the "Secret Service" man appears, shows the merchant forged I.D., and informs him that he's tracking down a new run of counterfeit that has appeared in the area, showing him the photocopy of the letter to substantiate this statement. Asking the merchant if he's taken in any hundred-dollar bills, he examines them. When he comes across the one his confederate used earlier, he picks it out and shows the merchant that the serial numbers match. He tells the merchant he must take the bill with him for "evidence."[4]

Another swindle having a revival is the "bank examiner" fraud. The fraud artist, posing as a "bank examiner," FBI agent, or other official, approaches his intended victim and asks him to cooperate in an investigation involving a dishonest teller at his bank. He asks the victim to withdraw a large sum of money from the bank and pass it on to the agent for "evidence," which will help to put the dishonest teller behind bars. The con artist tells the victim the Government will redeposit his money shortly, when the investigation is completed. He may even give the victim a receipt for the amount.[5]

All of these swindles work, and some work very well indeed. Some of them work only on very gullible victims, and others are so fool-proof they'll work on almost anyone. The bank examiner fraud seems to work best on the elderly, as they are the ones most often victimized, possibly because they come from an earlier, simpler era, when people appeared to be more honest.

NOTES

1. *Big Time Operator's Manual,* Scot Tinker, Eden Press, 1977.
2. *Crooks, Con Men, and Cheats,* Eugene Villiod, Gambler's Book Club, 1980, pp. 66-68.
3. *Clipping the Flocks,* Scot Tinker, Eden Press, 1977, p. 25.

4. *Professional Con-Games, Schemes, and Frauds,* Carl Dorski, Roadrunner Publications, 1979, pp. 12-13.

5. *Short Cons,* Scot Tinker, Eden Press, 1977, p. 7.

MOVING GOODS

Along with deceptive advertising, deceptive merchandising has been with us a long time. The line between them is hard to define, as is the line between legitimate business and fraud. Apart from "gimmicks" used to make the merchandize more attractive, there are financial incentives. We're so familiar with the phrase "for a limited time only" that often we don't even listen to it. We're also very familiar with "sales," as most stores have a "sale" of one sort or another every week.

While the "sales" offered by legitimate stores are real, in the sense that they are reductions of the established price, we ought to be wary of the reason behind them, and exactly how they work. They are "loss leaders," items which sell at little or no margin of profit, or even for lower than cost, in order to entice customers into the store. To make up for this, other items are overpriced. Indeed, it may even happen that the item on "sale" is available elsewhere for even less money.

When this happens, there's cause for suspicion that the item was not really on "sale" at all. False or inflated "list" prices are common gimmicks. In some areas, such as cameras and electronic equipment, "list" prices are unrealistically high, set that way so that the merchant can give the customer a "discount" every time.

Some glittering goods, usually cameras and jewelry found in stores located in tourist areas, come with several price tags apiece, so that the merchant can choose his preferred list price and claim to offer whatever discount he feels will be most effective.

There are also other gimmicks used to give the impression of a "sale." Wheedling phrases such as "made to sell for ...." imply that the value of the item is higher than it is, and that the merchant is discounting it. Keeping in mind that a legitimate sale price is one that's lower than the usual selling price, we find other goods being moved by the claim of "special introductory offer," which implies that, although the item has just come on the market and there is no base price for comparison, the selling price will go up after the "offer" is over, and of course the offer is "for a limited time only."

In most large cities there are certain areas that are full of "tourist traps." The Times Square area in New York is one, with each block lined with stores festooned with colorful signs proclaiming "sales." Many of these are "going out of business" sales and some are "going out of business today" sales. Some of these stores have been "going out of business" for several decades.[1]

Some of the "sales" are for items which the customer knows sell for much more elsewhere. It often happens that these prices are far below even wholesale, and the suspicion comes up that these must be stolen goods. More likely they are counterfeit or "seconds," defective goods. In many cities, there are stores that specialize in "seconds," lots of merchandise that do not meet the manufacturer's quality standards. Sometimes the defects are severe, but more often, as in clothing, the defects are such that the value and serviceability of the item is not reduced, as when the cut on a panel of clothing does not line up with the pattern of fabric.

Flea markets are excellent places for moving stolen goods as well as defective ones. These merchants, with shops that consist of collapsible tables, present an image like that of a Middle East bazaar. "Let the buyer beware" is certainly in force here. It's sometimes possible to detect defective material, but stolen goods carry another danger to the buyer. A good example is the flea market merchant who sold a top-of-the-line make of typewriter for one hundred dollars. These were not defective, just stolen, but yet a good deal for the buyer who did not question too closely. The problem would arise when the machine needed service or repair, because the manufacturer keeps a computerized file of all stolen machines, and requires the network of repair facilities to report all serial numbers of machines serviced to the central office. Whoever brought in such a machine might face charges of criminal receivership, unless he had a bill of sale to prove his purchase. Bills of sale are not common at flea markets. With luck, the buyer would only have to live with confiscation of the machine. Finding the merchant to recover the purchase price might be a problem.[2]

The surplus goods game is common, with many variants. Typically, the con artist, driving a truck and dressed appropriately, rings the doorbell. He explains that he had an order to deliver a load of fertilizer to someone down the street and that the buyer changed his mind. He adds that the load is not worth carting back, and that he's willing to sell it at cost or less to anyone who'll buy it. This story has many versions, and the material involved can be television sets and other appliances.

In moving goods, the "television game," although cumbersome, is one con that does not involve any actual appliances. The con man telephones an office, claiming to be the friend of a friend, and tells the listener that he can offer him television sets or other appliances that a local department store is selling as surplus for a very low price. He may try to hustle the sale by saying that the appliances are available only in small lots, and entice the listener into persuading several fellow employees to join in.

If the victim bites, the con man instructs him to meet him in the parking lot or the lobby of the store with the money. When the patsies show up, the fraud artist takes the money and instructs them to move their vehicles to the loading dock to collect the merchandise. The victims wait forever.[3]

The dangers of buying large-ticket items sight unseen are highlighted by the case of a furniture store that advertised "sale" items through the electronic media and the mail. This store used false list prices and misstated "sale" price, claimed that some sales were for "one day only" when they were not, substituted floor samples in their shipments, selling them as new, and shipped items different from those ordered.[4]

It pays to be suspicious of unusually good deals that seem to good to be true. They often are.

NOTES

1. Personal observation of author.

2. The stolen typewriter situation was explained to the author by a friend who is in the service business and who also attends flea markets regularly.

3. *Short Cons,* Scot Tinker, Eden Press, 1977. p. 8.

4. *Classic Mail Frauds,* Scot Tinker, Eden Press, 1977, p. 22.

PERSONAL DECEPTIONS

This section will start with a lighthearted deception before moving on to more serious ones. Occasionally, a man seeking to seduce a woman will, if he has the nerve, take her into a jewelry store on a Friday afternoon, immediately after the banks have closed. Buying a very expensive watch or piece of jewelry for her, he'll pay with a check. The salesman will point out to the couple that the store cannot release the merchandise, on a purchase of this size, until the check clears, and the soonest that can happen will be Monday. The couple, accepting this with good grace, leaves.

Monday, when the store employee calls the man to tell him there are not sufficient funds in his account to cover the check, the man replies; "I know, but thanks for the wonderful weekend!"[1]

The foregoing account sounds like a legend, the sort of story heard at a smoker, rather than a real case history. The following ones definitely *did* happen, and similar incidents continue to happen:

The hitchiker may not be what he seems. While we hear many cautions regarding the picking up of hitchikers, some are very attractive types, and behave properly once in the car. One such told the man who had picked him up that he was out of work, had run through his unemployment insurance, and was traveling on to try and find a job in a new town. The driver was very impressed with the young man's sincerity and clean-cut manner. He continued to question the young man, and found that he'd slept in a bus depot the previous night, and hadn't eaten that day.

They arrived in the driver's home town as night was falling, and the driver suggested that the young man come home with him to have supper, mentioning that his wife was a good cook. The young man appeared reluctant, not wanting to be a bother, and this convinced the driver further of the young man's sincerity and honesty. They proceeded to the driver's house, where the man's wife served them a satisfying supper. The young man seemed so well-mannered that they invited him to spend the night in the spare bedroom.

During the early hours of the morning, the driver woke up to find that the young man was gone, along with his wallet, money, and his car.[2]

The "business partner" scam can work in several different ways. In one instance, a man approached the victim, claiming he was in the jewelry business, but ill health made him devote less time than he should to running his business, and he was seeking a partner to help in the day-to-day affairs. The victim invited him home for supper, and during the meal the conversation turned to pieces of jewelry owned by the host's wife. The con man, upon seeing them, told her they were more valuable than she'd thought, and offered to take them to one of his business contacts for a formal appraisal. They turned over the jewelry to him, and he left. Several days later, when the victim wondered why he had not heard from the potential "business partner," he tried the phone number on the **business card the man had left, and found that it was a phoney. The man never returned.**[3]

The publisher of a struggling weekly newspaper hired a man who claimed he had over a million dollars in a Swiss account, which he'd be glad to invest in the newspaper to help it over the current crisis. There was one problem. To get the money out of his account, he had to appear in person in Switzerland, and he could not leave the country because he was on parole from prison. He had been in prison because of a conviction for fraud, a fact that the publisher, who surely thought himself to be a canny businessman, ignored.

The publisher hired him as an advertising salesman, or "Account Executive," and the con man sold a few ads while he supposedly worked on the problem of getting his funds out of Switzerland. He ran up large balances. on the newspaper's credit cards, made many international phone calls to "business contacts" and "lawyers" in both Europe and Hong Kong, all of them on the newspaper's lines. He floated around the office, telling anyone who had the time to listen about his impressive business deals and contacts in Europe, showing letterheads and business cards as substantiation of his claims.

The game eventually came to an end, as the publisher gradually realized that all he was going to get from this man was more bills and more excuses regarding the delay in the transfer of funds. By the time the publisher woke up to the fact that the ex-con he'd hired was milking him, he'd lost several thousand dollars.[4]

The "baby burglar" is an almost irresistable con, as most people are very compassionate regarding children. The doorbell rings, and when the householder opens the door there is a woman with a baby, who explains the baby is thirsty, shows an empty baby bottle, and asks for some water. The con woman, who may or may not be operating with a partner, uses the distraction to lift a wallet, purse, or any valuables that are easy to pocket.[5]

There are endless variations on the theme of using an excuse to gain admittance in order to commit a burglary. One woman was victimized by a person claiming to be a religious proselytizer. The victim let the other woman in, as she explained about her church and its doctrine. At one point, discussing the victim's work, they went into the bedroom, where the victim showed the woman a dress she was making. After the proselytizer had left, the victim noticed that her purse was missing.[6]

Once the con artist or burglar is in the home, there are all sorts of distractions and dodges to get the victim out of the room so he may "toss" the room and "lift" whatever is easy to take. If the victim offers a cup of coffee, that gives an opportunity of several minutes' duration. Asking to use the bathroom is an almost foolproof way, as few victims will accompany the con artist through the house to the door of the bathroom, unless the layout of the house is so complicated that the bathroom is truly hard to find.

If the telephone is in another room, an accomplice can phone the victim, getting him or her out of the room for a short while. A request to use the phone, on the other hand, is a door-opener. It's hard to resist someone who claims to have had a car breakdown and who asks to call for help. Sometimes, the phone call can serve as a cover for a theft by stealth, but at other times the crime is violent.

What many people with unlisted numbers don't realize is how easy it is to find out the number, even without the "friend in the phone company" so often cited in the "how-to" books and detective novels. A request to use the phone to cope with an emergency will almost always produce results. The conventional advice to homeowners is never to admit anyone, but to ask for the number they wish to contact and place the call themselves. This will prevent a burglary, but will disclose the unlisted number if the number the con man provides is that of an accomplice, supposedly the owner of a garage. He tells the person calling that it will take a couple of minutes to contact a tow truck on the radio, and asks for the phone number so that he may call back.

NOTES

1. *Clipping the Flocks,* Scot Tinker, 1977, Eden Press, p. 17.

2. *A Compendium of Bunk,* Carey and Sherman, 1976. Charles C. Thomas, pp. 56-58.

3. Ibid., p. 59.

4. Personal acquaintance of the author.

5. *A Compendium of Bunk,* p. 61.

6. Ibid.,pp. 61-2.

PERSONAL IMPROVEMENT

There is a whole category of groups and services that fall loosely under "personal improvements." These do not train in job-related skills, but in ways that enhance the way a person feels about him or herself.

The first we'll consider is part of what we might call the "Fear Industry." It's true, the crime rate is at an all-time high, and street crime in America gets a lot of publicity. It's also true that the fear of crime that grips a lot of people gets extensive coverage in the news. Given this, it's no surprise that many store-front "schools" have sprung up to teach various forms of self defense, from karate and other types of hand-to-hand combat to techniques of handling firearms for personal protection. Some of the instructors are competent. Most are not, as the motive is quick profits, not high-quality instruction. This is especially true in firearms instruction, for unlike the karate schools, there is no national association, no system of accreditation, and no set of standards that they must meet to qualify as self-defense schools.

Usually, the trappings and atmosphere are designed to pass the instructor off as a "tough guy" who can handle himself in any situation. Often, the instructor wears camouflage clothing and has a pistol tucked into his belt, as if expecting an imminent attack. He may claim to be a former Green Beret, or policeman, as qualification for teaching firearms defense. He may have gotten all of his shooting experience from competition in "Combat Matches," which differ seriously from conditions on the street. Often, the shooting techniques the instructor teaches are more suited to competition than the street.

As cost is a factor, the courses often are short, giving the student very little. As with any skill, it takes time to develop proficiency, and even the best and most dedicated instructor can do only so much. If the operator of the school is dishonest, he'll promise more than he can deliver, claiming to be able to make the student the equal of any street situation in just a few weeks of part-time instruction.

One school offered a course labelled "ranger training," designed supposedly for the survivalist or paramilitary type. Unfortunately, the students did not even get the level of "training" of the "weekend warriors," the National Guard, as they had class only on Sunday afternoon, during which the instructor taught them how to fight the Vietnam War over again. Possibly none of the students realized that it takes much more time than a few Sunday afternoons to turn a young person in good physical shape into a Ranger.

A few years ago, "sensitivity training" was the fad. There were various versions of "sensitivity training" offered by "psychologists" and various "institutes" around the country, all at high prices. These "encounter groups" would hold regular meetings during which the members were encouraged to bare their deepest feelings, the process sometimes aided by a requirement of total nudity.

The alleged "benefits" of this sort of experience were often unclear, with each "institute" and street-corner psychologist peddling his own version. What they all had in common was a high price. Like other types of group affairs, such as smoking and weight loss clinics, their results vary. As in every sort of therapy group, there are certain principles of group dynamics that apply.

There is always a group "leader." He may be the "therapist," "guru," or have some other title, but his job is to direct the group overtly.

There usually is a small number of supporters in the group and these may be called "assistant leaders" or some other titles, or they may not be overt at all, but blending in with members of the group to perform the same functions as "shills."

It's a well known fact that most people are conformists to a certain degree. To make people do a certain thing, it's usually very helpful to show them that others are doing it, too. An example is the disrobing that takes place in some "encounter" groups. When the leader gives the command to disrobe, any who hesitate will see others taking their clothes off quickly, without hesitancy or embarrassment.

A fashionable term for this phenomenon is "peer pressure." It is the same thing seen in the "brainwashing" practiced in some countries. The threat of disapproval of the group serves to keep individualistic or deviant individuals in line. It works the same way in groups in this country. The groups offer certain personality changes. The effect comes about by peer pressure and conformism to the attitudes and expectations of the group.

We might legitimately ask, at this point, whether it matters how the effect comes about, as long as it gives the participants what they're seeking. It does matter. Changes produced by the influence of the group can, and often do, reverse themselves after the participant leaves the group. There may be very gratifying effects at the moment, but some months later the ex-member may be asking himself what he got out of it.

It's important to note that these group dynamics apply to all groups, whether they involve mind improvement of a sort, weight reduction, psychotherapy, smoking groups, etc.

Many of these groups depend on the fact that most states do not regulate "counselors," as we've seen in the section on health care. Anyone can put himself into practice as a marriage counselor, psychotherapist, or even "group therapist."[1]

Sex therapy has become a fad in recent years. Without a doubt, some of it is legitimate, but some are scams. Some are thin covers for prostitution operations, with clients being given "sex therapy" to "cure" them of a "problem." Perhaps these are the least harmful of the category, as they provide a certain service for a certain price, and that is that.

Others, the ones that claim to "treat" various psychosexual disorders, can do a lot of harm. As with other types of health care, it's difficult to prove that doctors with legitimate medical degrees and licenses do any better, and one of the most obvious facts is that the legitimate practitioners disagree on methods of treatment for psychosexual disorders. However, there is no doubt about the motives of the fraudulent operator.

Some of these operators cater to some of the kinkiest desires, and even gratify them for themselves. Asking couples to have intercourse while the "therapist" watches may be helpful in some cases, but in others it may just satisfy the "therapist's" Peeping-

Tom impulses. Some clients may unwittingly be modeling for pornographic films and tapes, shot by cameras which may or may not be hidden.[2] Sometimes, there is more than one source of profit for the operator.

Understandably, complaints to the police are far fewer than the number of operators would justify. A man seeking "therapy" for impotence is not likely to be eager to discuss his problem with the police, even if he's been bilked. It may even be that he's already been unsuccessfully treated by an M.D. before he decided to place his trust in a "sex therapist."

NOTES

1. *Clipping The Flocks,* Scot Tinker, Eden Press, 1977, pp. 19-20.
2. Ibid., p. 19.

PERSONAL PROPERTY

A way that some con men raise quick cash is to sell the victim a piece of personal property at an attractive price, get payment, or at least an installment, in cash, and then leave town. Some of these schemes may seem simple-minded, but in fact many people fall for them.

One technique is selling a fake diamond by representing it as real. The diamond is usually set into a piece of jewelry, and the fraud artist and the victim go to the jeweler's to have it appraised. The jeweler is often totally innocent and unrelated to the con game. The con man may even encourage the mark to pick a jeweler whom he trusts.

The jeweler appraises the diamond, confirming that it is worth what the con man claims it is. At the first opportunity afterwards, the con man makes the "switch." It is easy for him to do, as he can rightfully retain possession of the jewelry until the mark pays him for it, and it's a simple matter to have a copy of the piece of jewelry in the same pocket as the real one.[1]

A variation on this theme is for the hustler to present the mark with a written appraisal showing that the jewelry is worth much more than the asking price, and offering to accompany the victim to a local jeweler to have it appraised once again. The second appraisal is supposedly for the victim's "protection," but it also gives the fraud artist an opportunity to make the "switch." Once he collects the money, he's gone.[2]

There is a scheme called "block laying" that involves passing off cheap merchandise as very valuable material.[3] It is also adaptable to selling stolen merchandise. The tactic is to make a purchase, leaving the piece of personal property as security. The con man can tell a service station attendant that he lost his wallet, needs some gas and perhaps a new battery to get where he's going, and offers to leave his watch as security for the amount he buys. He can dress up his story by claiming to be a member of a musical group and promising the attendant free tickets to the performance, etc.

A nervy, but effective way to raise quick cash is for the fraud artist to sell a rented car. The simplest way for the swindler to do this is to rent a car using a forged credit card, the same one he uses to pay for his hotel or motel room. He then advertises the car for sale at a very attractive price. He can save time, if he does this regularly, by phoning in the ad before he has the car or even before he arrives in town, as usually he can reserve a car and knows which model and make it will be.

When the calls come in, he arranges to meet a prospect in a parking lot near his home. The story he tells him is the crux of the fraud, and the swindler must deliver it in a convincing manner. He tells his mark that there has just been a death in the family, that he's willing to sell the car at a low price to raise quickly the money to fly back home, and that a small deposit, say five hundred dollars, will enable him to turn the car over to the mark. He promises to have his lawyer send the necessary papers for a formal bill of sale and transfer of title, and asks the victim to drive him to the airport.[4]

There is a variant on this method, which enables the con artist to profit several times from selling the same car. This also works with a rental car. The basic idea is have forged papers for the car, sell it to the mark, and then steal it back, reselling it the next day.[5] There are some items of window dressing that can go along with the basic technique.

One way is for the fraud artist to be a female. To anyone who answers the ad, she can claim that her husband has just left her, thrown her out, etc., and that she's selling the car to get some ready cash. She can also assume the role of having just lost her job, being unable to afford the rent, and needing cash to be allowed to remain in her apartment.

Stealing the car back is the easiest part. In order to sell the car to so many people, the swindler needs some sets of duplicate keys, and he or she uses one set to repossess the car each night.

If the swindler is using forged papers, he can even use his own car for the sale, as he's going to take it back at the end, anyway. It requires some fine judgement, though, to know when to stop running this scam in one location, as the repetition of stolen auto complaints to the police, all involving the same make and model of car, will sooner or later attract attention.

NOTES

1. *A Compendium of Bunk,* Carey and Sherman, 1976, Charles C. Thomas, p. 141.

2. *Professional Con Games, Schemes, and Frauds,* Carl Dorski, 1979, Roadrunner Publications, p. 7.

3. *Short Cons,* Scot Tinker, Eden Press, 1977, p. 26.

4. Ibid., p. 25.

5. Ibid., p. 37.

PLAYING ON HOPES

There are scams that play on people's hopes, and they cross the lines between categories. Some of them are postal frauds, and others perhaps belong in the "income" category. They all use the same basic mechanism. An advertisement appeals to the person who thinks he has talent, and promises help in developing that talent, and make contacts in the field so that the "talented" person may find employment using that talent.

One fraud started out as a "contest" for lyric writers. Each person who sent an entry received a letter telling him or her that he or she had won, and definitely had talent. Along with the encouraging letter comes a contract, the "prize," which for a fee promises the talent agency will have a music writer compose a tune for the lyrics, a performer will sing the song, and the result will be presented to the decision-makers of various famous recording companies.[1]

"Talent agencies" also victimize singers. One amateur answered an ad placed by such a "talent agency" and found that if he handed over several hundred dollars for "expenses" he could perform accompanied by several musicians and have his performance recorded on tape. The tape would then go to the head of a recording company, and he'd be on his way to stardom.[2] The operator of this "talent agency" collected as much money as he could from aspiring singers, then moved out of his opulent office, sending back the rented furniture.

"Model agencies" are another scam. There are legitimate ones, but there are also the operators who prey on aspiring models. These scams also start off with an ad, sometimes for a "talent contest," and sometimes with a promise to develop the person's "talent." They always ask for a fee, for "expenses." While a reputable agency will, for example, suggest the aspiring model should have a portfolio, the client is free to choose his or her photographer and have the work done elsewhere. The fraud artist will tell the client that the agency has its own photographer and printer, and even offer a "discount." The hit-and-run con man will collect the money and skip out, leaving the clients high and dry. Others will lead the clients along for quite a time, making a profit from the photography and printing, then suggesting the client needs "coaching" to develop the talent. Of course, the agency will be glad to supply the coaching for a price. The fraudulent part is that the agency makes no effort to contact potential users of that talent, as promised. Some operators are quite skilled at stringing their clients along, telling them they are not quite ready for presentation, and some additional "coaching" will move them another step towards their goal.[3]

The important point to note, for anyone with talent, is that reputable and honest agents do not charge fees. They work on commission, collecting a percentage of whatever the performer earns. The same is true of publishers and literary agents. Legitimate publishers pay royalties or buy the work outright, and never charge the author for "editing" and other "expenses." Any agency that demands money "up front" from an aspirant is likely to be a fraud.

NOTES

1. *A Compendium of Bunk,* Carey and Sherman, Charles C. Thomas, 1976, pp. 168-170.

2. Ibid., pp. 163-168.

3. Ibid., pp. 170.

POSTAL FRAUDS

Fraud using the mails has become almost an institution in this and other countries. It is not confined to buying goods sight unseen and later finding out they are defective, but to many schemes of such subtlety and complexity that it's impossible to cover them all in one book.

Unlike the telephone company, the Postal Service is an arm of the government and maintains a staff of Postal Inspectors to police the use and misuse of the mails.[1]

Deceptive advertisements are perhaps the simplest form of mail fraud. Some operators cheat the client by not sending the merchandise, and by the time the complaints pour in and the Postal Inspectors come around, they've left town.

Such an operator will probably use a "mail drop," a fake address, not a post office box. Renters of post office boxes must list their correct names and addresses, and it's a crime to use an assumed name. Privately operated mail drops follow no such restrictions, and the operator's main concern is that the client pay his bill. A P.O. box contract runs for six months, while a mail drop rents for whatever the operator and client agree. The charge for a P.O. box of the smallest size is typically around ten dollars for each six-month period, while mail drops go for about nine dollars a month. Prices for mail drops vary widely, and there are special services available, such as remailing, at an extra charge.

The next category is the deceptive ad which promises more than the operator delivers. One common type, used over the years, is the one which promises a system of earning money which will make the client rich very quickly. Without telling the reader exactly what the system is, and often telling nothing at all, the ad promises him great success for a very minimal effort and investment. The sucker who sends in his ten or twenty dollars usually gets a booklet detailing an unworkable scheme, often involving a mail-order business.

Some ads promise to pay the reader. One, for a hair loss cure, promised to pay the reader five dollars to test the product.

Reading the fine print on this full-page ad revealed that the reader first had to buy the product, paying $24.75, and the company would pay him five dollars only if he continued to use the product for sixty days and reported favorable results.[2]

The fake vacation coupon is a winner for the con man. A four-color ad appears, offering the reader a chance to win a free vacation in a contest if he'll send in the coupon. Each person who responds gets a letter telling him or her that he won the trip, an all-expense paid vacation in Hawaii or some other well-known place. However, there is a fee to secure the reservation and pay for mailing and handling costs. Those who send in the fee will find when the time comes for them to go on their vacation, some months later, that there is no trip, and the office has "moved," if it ever was there.[3]

Some people are leery of replying to a P.O. box. This caution is only partly justified, because private mail drops often have street addresses, which masks their true purpose. The reader may send in his money feeling a false confidence in the stability or legitimacy of the "company."

Another aspect that should be obvious is that in the real world nobody gives something for nothing, and this fact is obscured by cleverly worded ads that are designed to give the impression that Santa Claus has just arrived. Readers may find it hard to believe how much time and effort go into designing and wording the ads, the effect calculated to mask the fact that there is really no free lunch. One man stated that he usually took ninety days to design an ad, and that he'd go over it every day, word by word, in an effort to make it perfect before he inserted it in a publication.[4]

A variation on the vacation con was a group that operated under the name of an automobile club, and sent to purchasers of new cars letters offering them vacation gift certificates, good for all expenses, at various resort areas. The letter requested an eighteen dollar "service" fee.[5]

Yet another variant is the coupon book fraud, which may be for vacation areas or for local merchants. Some offers for books of "discount" coupons are legitimate, in the sense that the purchaser actually gets a book of coupons that the merchant will honor, but others are strictly bogus, with the buyer getting a book of counterfeits or nothing at all. In any event, the buyer should be aware that merchants who "give" discounts are not seeking to lose money, and often jack up the prices to permit "discounts" and "rebates."

Sometimes the fraud appeals to the victim's ego. One operator did not advertise, but used a commercial mailing list, sending each potential victim a letter telling him he was qualified for a listing in the local *Who's Who*. The letter informed the recipient he could purchase a copy of the book for a fee and that it would be sent to him upon publication. The swindler collected the money, but never had any books printed.[6]

Lonely-hearts clubs, computer-assisted or not, operate through the mails as well as face-to-face. However, some lonely-hearts victimizers offer spurious marriage proposals, extracting money in the process. One gambit is worked by a writer claiming to be female and played upon a lonely man. She offers to join him, if he'll send her money to cover her expenses in moving. She's always 'a resident in another far-away state for this to work, and in reality the writer may not even be female.

It also works the other way, with females being victimized by these gigolos-by-mail. Sometimes, the game is that the man asks the woman to invest in a business, or even to open a joint bank account.[7]

One widespread, but little-documented, area of fraud has to do with "swinger's" and other sexually-oriented clubs. The simplest ploy is for a "swinger's" magazine to have a classified ad section, in which readers place their ads seeking contacts. It's general practice for the listers not to have their names and addresses in the ads, but rather a box number care of the publication. The publication will accept and forward mail addressed to a box number, providing that the sender encloses a forwarding fee. In effect, the publication operates as a letter drop. There is no way to establish how many of the ads are legitimate and how many are spurious, inserted by the operator of the publication to stimulate traffic. The person who sends the letter off to a number at the magazine's office, not knowing who the ultimate addressee is, has no guarantee that the person placing the ad, even if it is a legitimate ad, will want to answer.

The forwarding fee racket is only one of the scams that plague this sort of publication's readers. At least as common is the advertisement placed under false pretenses.

Some ads specify that the respondent must send a photo. In fact, some state boldly; "No reply without photo." In this context, "photo" means a photograph showing the genital area. Without a doubt, some ads are placed by sincere persons. Others are devices used by those who collect photos to add to their collections. Anyone who sends a nude photo with the initial reply to such an ad is taking a chance of having the photo wind up in some collection and perhaps being reproduced and passed around the country among members of the subculture that exchange such photos. Of course, there will be no reply.

One reason so many of those who place sexually-oriented ads use mail drops, even if they are legitimate, is because of the prospect of blackmail. Sending off a letter describing such personal details as sexual performances and practices to a stranger is risky at best, and if the recipient is running a blackmail racket, the outcome can be disastrous. Because of the underground nature of this sexual subculture, and the understandable reluctance of blackmail victims to report to the authorities, we'll never know the extent of this practice.

We can, however, make a guess that it is becoming less common. In recent years, a much greater proportion of the ads listed street addresses, phone numbers, and names. With the loosening up of sexual morality, and more widespread acceptance of practices that would have been cause for ostracism a decade ago, fewer sexual nonconformists find it necessary to hide their identities. A blackmailer would find it difficult to intimidate a person who does not care who knows of his or her sexual habits, and even may flaunt them, as by participation in a "Gay Pride" parade, complete with television coverage by Action News.

Nevertheless, there are many opportunities for deception with sexually-oriented ads. We can judge that this is a serious problem, and even estimate the nature of the types of deceptions, by the exasperated phrases that appear often in such ads:

"No fats, fems, or drugs."

"No hippies or kinky stuff."

"Only sincere replies."

We can infer that some who respond to such ads are less than candid about their physical states or their practices. A person expecting a sexual contact from a response to an ad might not have formed an accurate impression of the respondent from the details revealed in the correspondence, and might be surprised to find that instead of a slim, youthful figure, the contact is aged and grossly overweight. Similarly, a contact seeker may be dismayed to find the second party has a drug habit.

Another area of trouble lies in what's covered by the word "kinky." While there are all sort of sexual preferences and practices, some are unusual indeed, and appear bizarre to the uninitiated. In the case of the sadomasochistic variants, they may seem not only bizarre, but are actually painful. Some who specialize in "genitorture," as it is known in the trade, will be quite forward about their preference. One such ad stated quite unequivocally: "Into heavy leather, S/M top....piercing and torture a specialty. Have full complement of toys."

There is nothing misleading about the wording of the fore-going ad, and anyone can tell what to expect. Others, however, are not so explicit, and misunderstandings result.

Some advertisers seek permanent relationships, and this can lead to complications, even when the participants are both sincere. When one or the other is practicing deception, problems inevitably result, and the only variable is how long it takes for the victim to realize that he's being had.

An ad that begins: "Seek young lady (or lad) to share home with older man...." will get all sorts of responses. It's inevitable that there will be an exchange of photos, which may be real or not. The ad may be a come-on placed by a photo collector, or it may be for the purpose of attracting sexually explicit letters.

Sometimes, the ad will go on to state the advertiser will help pay relocation expenses. This statement, in an ad, will attract a reply from every person out to make a dishonest buck. The game works the same way whether the relationship is heterosexual, homosexual, or of another category. The respondent sends a description that is appealing, and perhaps a photograph to back it up. It's an obvious fact that the letter may be totally false, and even written by someone of the opposite sex. Similarly, the enclosed photograph need not be of the letter writer. The respondent may indeed have collected some suitable photographs by placing a similar ad himself.

As the letter game develops, the "young person" pleads poverty, and may claim to be out of work. This can serve as an excuse for not having a phone or not contacting by long-distance. It also sets the stage for extracting money for "moving" expenses. The con artist, who "lives" several states away, has no job to tie him to the area, no great amount of personal possessions to add to the "moving" expenses, and appears to be a good deal for the older victim.

There are endless possibilities on the "moving expenses" game. Limited only by the victim's patience and gullibility, the fraud artist can extract several payments over several weeks' time. The first can be for "gas money" to enable the applicant to make the trip. After receipt of the first payment, the con man can come back and inform the sucker that his car needs repair, and to please send more money.

Yet another variation on the "moving in together" theme is a deception played by the placer of the ad. Posing as an older, established person, he places an ad claiming to seek a live-in partner, all expenses paid. Responding only to those in the local area, he'll meet them and inititate a sexual contact, possibly paying for a dinner along the way. The contacts somehow never seem to work out to permanent relationships, because the advertiser just wants to touch and taste, and is not seeking a permanent relationship, but a different partner every night.

In this sort of "affair" it often happens that the deception is not all on one side, and the initial contact need not come through the mails. It's naive to believe that an attractive young person would be eager to start a relationship with an older one, at first sight unseen, out of love and devotion. Often, the real objective for the impoverished aspirant is simply a meal ticket.

Some relatively harmless ads in sexually-oriented publications are placed by "writers" who claim to be collecting "case histories" for an article or a book regarding some aspect of sex. Anyone who writes to them will find that these "writers" will ask them for very explicit details of their sexual practices, but will be very unspecific regarding when the article or book is due to appear, being unable to state who the publisher is. In fact, the "writers" are part of a very small sexual subculture that collects personally written pornography, prefering that to the hack-written porn that appears in commercial publications.

A variation on this theme appears in an ad that begins:

"Successful Free lance photographer...." and goes on to state: "Tell me your secret sex fantasy in your first letter — and please include a revealing photograph of yourself." Apart from wondering why a "photographer" would be soliciting photographs, it's hard to tell what the motivation behind this ad is.

A variation of postal fraud that has nothing to do with sex is the sort of advertisement for "mercenaries" that appears in the "armchair macho" magazines, especially the ones that supposedly are aimed at "professional adventurers" and the like. The classified ad sections contain advertisements for "mercenaries," stating that there are jobs open for those interested in becoming mercenary soldiers, and offering "free" details. The advertiser claims to be a clearinghouse or employment agency for mercenaries, and the applicant finds out that, for a fee, he'll be told whom to contact for such employment.

Several angry letters protesting these "rip-offs" have been published in the letters-to-the-editor columns of these magazines, telling of the disappointing experiences that some applicants had had at the hands of these advertisers. Often, the fee would be twenty-five or fifty dollars, and the only reply would be an address in a foreign country. A letter to that address would produce no reply, and follow-up letters to the "clearinghouse" would not be answered. Prosecution was hindered by the fact that some of these advertisers were in foreign countries, and we've already seen that prosecution across national lines is very difficult.

Another type of advertisement appearing in the "armchair macho" magazine offers instruction by mail in the various military skills needed to become a mercenary. There were no letters to the editors denouncing these rip-offs, and we can assume that those who sent in their money did get something back for it. The value of what they got is open to question. We've already seen the instruction in various store-front "martial arts" and "para-military and survival" schools is questionable at best, and that it simply isn't possible to train someone to be a soldier of any sort in weekly Sunday afternoon sessions.

Those who employ mercenaries recruit from individuals who have seen service in an established elite unit, such as the SAS, Foreign Legion, etc., and who have combat experience. Any expectation that they would take seriously a certificate from a correspondence school for mercenaries is wildly optimistic, at best. Such instruction is in the same class as that offered by the mail-order schools for "detectives."

There are endless variations of mail frauds employed, and the swindlers think up new ones, or new wrinkles on old ones, every day. Some of these fraud artists show great ingenuity, and often their efforts go well rewarded. Crime does pay!

NOTES

1. The Postal Inspectors will usually respond promptly to **complaints of mail fraud, as the Post Office takes responsibility for** the use to which people put the U.S. Mail. The Postal Inspectors originally were established to combat mail robbers, but their role has changed over the years.

The performance of the Postal Inspectors in contrast to that of the enforcement arm of the telephone company is painfully apparent to anyone who has had any dealings with both. The frustration experienced by someone who tries to report something as simple as an obscene phone call is typical of what the telephone client can expect from the "security officers" of the phone company. In reality, the telephone company is not interested in what use or misuse a client may make of his telephone, as long as he pays his bill.

2. *Arizona Republic*, March 21, 1984.

3. *A Compendium of Bunk,* Carey and Sherman, 1976, Charles C. Thomas, pp. 127-128.

4. Author's interview with a mail swindler.

5. *Classic Mail Frauds,* Scot Tinker, Eden Press, 1977.

6. Ibid., p. 31.

7. *Clipping The Flocks,* Scot Tinker, Eden Press, 1977, p. 16.

REAL ESTATE FRAUDS

Con artists selling worthless parcels of land and promoting various forms of real estate sight unseen have been with us for centuries. There is no documentation of the earliest such frauds, but we can assume that real estate swindles are truly classic. Probably the earliest ones in this country occurred during the last two centuries, which virtually covers the history of the United States. **Phoney gold mines were popular during the Nineteenth** Century, after the gold rush. The con man would sell a piece of land, or an actual digging, on which he claimed gold existed to be mined. In cases of skeptical buyers, the con man would make a small investment and buy some gold nuggets, with which he would "seed" the area and invite the prospective buyer for an inspection. "Seeding" a "mine" is a very convincing way to persuade a victim the land has value, and will fool anyone but an expert.

The Twentieth Century brought with it another variety of real estate fraud, the "vacation" or "investment" swindle. Florida was the site of a boom in land swindles during the 1920's, with con men buying swampland or tidal land and selling it sight unseen to buyers in other states. While this became a scandal at the time, new generations have come on the scene, and with them new swindlers, and the practice goes on, under different names and in different places.[1]

Arizona was the site of many such frauds in recent years. The operators would sell their victims parcels of land that were out in the desert, almost inaccessible and with no fresh water or any utilities. Some of these parcels were on mountain peaks, but anyone buying them sight unseen would not know this.

While there are today some instances of swindlers selling property they do not own, faking the documentation and leaving town with the money before the victim finds out, this is outright, indictable fraud, which the smart operator tries to avoid because it leaves him wide-open to prosecution.[2]

Falsifying papers to a piece of land the swindler does not even own is possible, with little effort, but its success depends on hustling relatively unsophisticated people, obtaining the money before they have time to check it out, and leaving as quickly as possible. Often, there won't be an outright sale, but just a request for a "deposit," or an advance on the "closing costs." The swindler convinces the victim he has a pressing reason for settling the deal quickly, and as the amount is not very great, and the total price very attractive, the victim pays willingly. The asking price can be extremely attractive, as the swindler is not selling the land and does, in fact, not even own it.

A variation on this theme occurs when the swindler notifies his victims they have "won" a parcel of land in a lottery or contest. He requests a nominal sum for "closing costs" on pieces of real estate that he does not own, or perhaps do not even exist.

With increased awareness of fraudulent land sales, and a tightening of laws pertaining to real estate transactions, the swindlers had to find new ways to sell property. Instead of the crude device of offering parcels that they did not own, they took to buying worthless land cheaply and inflating its value by selling dreams.

The operator would buy a large parcel of land, usually worthless but quite legitimate, and build a model home or two on it. Hiring an artist to draw up renditions of other homes, shopping centers, and recreational facilities, the swindler would promote this land to unsuspecting prospects. He would show them the drawings, and tout the property as a developing area with each piece of real estate appreciating in value over the next few years. In fact, the only appreciation would be the inflated price tag put on by the swindler himself, and any buyer who tried to unload his land later would have a hard time even finding another buyer, let alone collecting his price back.

Usually, the fraudulent sales presentations take place in a party-like atmosphere, with many people getting invitations by mail to attend the land offering. There will be refreshments, and the crowd will be laced by a few "shills," the swindler's confederates who will ostentatiously sign contracts for parcels and announce to the others they thought it was a terrific deal.

In some operations, there is an additional incentive. The operator offers his prospects the choice of an outright sale or an "opportunity" to get their parcels free if they find other buyers.

The operator may keep the ball rolling by renting some mobile homes and placing them on lots on the "development" to give the impression of growing sales. In some cases, he'll have his shills play the role of buying property from the first victims in order to develop a small corps of legitimate buyers who feel the "deal" is worthwhile and profitable, and will recommend it to their friends. Thusly, an operator who paid ten dollars for a parcel of land can sell it for several thousand dollars by investing in some minimal "improvements" and laying out some "front money" for his shills. In some instances, the wheeling and dealing can become quite convoluted, with the operator using other people's money and reaping his profit at each stage.[3]

The key to selling such real estate rip-offs is setting the atmosphere, and in some cases this preparation can be very elaborate. One source[4] cites such a scene, in which the fraud artist approaches a couple on vacation, flatters them, gives them tickets to a show, and ends up by inviting them to a party on a yacht the next day. He tells them that the party is really a business meeting regarding a deal that need not concern them, and they should just enjoy the ride.

On the yacht, the master of ceremonies calls the meeting to order and begins to describe a land "deal" to a group of "investors." Some of them, the operator's shills, raise objections, but during the proceedings show they are convinced the "deal" is a good investment. Of course, the victims can't help but hear the presentation, and slowly get the idea that perhaps they, too, might profit from the "deal."

When the con man who approached them the day before sits down next to them and tells them that although he knows they are not interested in the "deal," it is a good investment for those who have enough money to buy the large blocks of land being offered. If they show the slightest flicker of interest, he continues to describe the virtues of the "deal" and the profits that an investor can earn. If he senses they are biting, he tells them although the land is for sale only in large blocks, he'll talk to the man in charge and see if he'd be willing to release a small lot for his "friends." Inevitably, the man in charge is only too happy to release a small lot the couple can afford, and they sign a contract, pay the initial amount, and finance the rest.

Some of these operators seem to invest a lot of money in promoting their schemes. In some instances, they will even fly their intended victims to the site of the land, and despite the obvious fact the land is desolate, many victims buy on the strength of the con man's personality and the promise of development and appreciating value.[5]

Although driving or flying the marks to the site seems to be an unnecessary expense, there are certain advantages to this. Transporting the victims away from their familar surroundings aids the con game, because it isolates them from friends and neighbors who might walk in to interrupt the proceedings, and forestalls them from picking up the phone to seek advice from a lawyer. Placing them in a group setting and using shills to manipulate the atmosphere is a clever use of the principles of group psychology, and we have already noted that con artists, although they may lack some formal education, are street-wise masters of practical psychology.

Turning to a fringe area, we find the "block-busters." They usually work in cities, concentrating their operations in neighborhoods that are changing in ethnic composition. Usually, the block busters are legitimate real estate agencies, promoting their business by using scare tactics.

In most cities, there are neighborhoods in which ethnic populations are entering. The block busters will canvass a block, telling each resident who answers the door that an ethnic family has bought a house down the block, or around the corner, and this will drive property values down. He offers to buy the house, usually for significantly less than the appraised value, and urges the owners to sell before it is too late. This process is exactly the reverse of the other sort of land swindle. Instead of promising an increase in value as an incentive to buy, the block buster promises a decrease in value as an incentive to sell.

Often the block buster is aided in his efforts by an ethnic family who actually moves into the area, for all of the other residents to observe. Inevitably, this will cause some of the homeowners to panic, and the real estate operator can play on their fears and pick up their property cheaply. He then resells it to other ethnic families, who are willing to pay his price because from their viewpoint, they are entering a better neighborhood than they left.

It's a misconception to think the only people who are taken in by land frauds are the stupid and unsophisticated ones. On the contrary, some frauds are designed to appeal to professionals. The "Land Paper" scheme is one.

Doctors, dentists, and other professionals often have money to invest, and indeed many of them are seeking tax shelters. The land paper artist does not sell land, but sales contracts to land at a discount. The con artist pretends to be from a well-known investment firm, and informs the doctor that it is holding paper on land which it wants to unload to make other investments. He promises a fat return, and a tax shelter. As an added inducement, he offers the doctor an option to buy stock in the company at a discount, adding that, although the company expects the value of its stock to go up during the next few months, even if the price remains the same the doctor will have made a profit because of the discounted purchase price.

If the doctor bites, he'll get payments from the company for a few months, and he may refer some of his fellow professionals to the company. Shortly thereafter, he'll find his dividend checks stopping, and when he attempts to contact the salesman he finds the office has moved, leaving no forwarding address. If he investigates further, he'll find the well-known company has no knowledge of the salesman or the land paper he sold the doctor.[6]

This is a variation on the Ponzi Game. The con artist knows that doctors have a lot of money, that they are interested in tax shelters and also earning more money, and that professionals in any community are a tightly-knit group, especially vulnerable to a Ponzi Scheme. If one bites, he'll recommend others, and the pack will follow the leader. In this respect, doctors are no more canny or resistant to victimization than their less-educated patients.

One type of real estate fraud that requires little investment from the con man and little time to carry out is the false rental. Basically, the fraud artist rents out property that belongs to someone else.

He gains control of the apartment or house by renting it from a legitimate landlord. He then advertises it himself, and rents it to all who are willing, establishing an occupancy date far enough into the future to enable him to swindle several other victims.[7]

A variation on this theme is to rent a property in a vacation area, and proceed to rent it out to many others. This practice solves two problems for the con man:

It permits him to rent the property sight unseen, to people who don't live in the area. This eliminates the possibility of the real owners seeing the ad in his local paper and becoming suspicious.

Usually, people rent a vacation cabin or apartment many months in advance, which gives the con man a comfortable margin during which he can rent the same property to as many people as he can inveigle.[8]

A legal version of the rental ploy is the "roommate" angle. The con man rents a luxury apartment with a lease that permits him to sub-let. He then advertises for a couple of girls to live in the luxury apartment, earning a small salary and free rental with the understanding that they would be "friendly." He then advertises for two men to share an apartment with two girls, at a rental that earns him a fat profit.[9]

A swindle that requires only a briefcase, some blank leases, and a convincing manner is the "new owner" swindle. The con man selects an apartment building and rings the doorbells a few days before the end of the month. He informs each tenant the building has a new owner. He explains the new owner has been concerned about the apartment manager, and he asks some questions about him, requesting that they keep the matter confidential because there was a possibility of replacing him.

At this point, the con man brings out a blank lease, and tells the tenant the new rent will be less than he had been paying. He requests the first and last month's rent, and leaves them a copy of the lease.[10]

The "rent skimmer" is another type who rents out property he doesn't own. He works in at least two ways:

The first is to make a deposit on a house as if he were going to buy it. If he can get control of the keys this way, he can show the house to prospective tenants and "rent" it to them as if he were the real owner.

The first method works even better when the rent skimmer is a sales agent for a development. As the agent, he has the keys and control of the properties. As it often takes a year or more for all of the houses in a development to sell, the skimmer can rent out the unsold and unoccupied ones on short-term rentals, and pick up enough money to supplement his commissions very amply.

The second method is to gain control of the property by seeking out houses which are about to be foreclosed. When he finds one, he offers to buy the property from the harried owner at an attractive price, offering a very small payment as "earnest money." The success of this scheme depends on the fact that there is usually a delay of several months between the initial transaction and the closing of a house purchase, and there is also a delay until repossession takes place on a foreclosure. The con man spends the time well, renting the house to as many as he can and disappearing with the money before the dates come up.[11]

There is an endless variety of real estate frauds, and part of the reason they succeed is people place too much trust in a real estate deal, perhaps feeling because they are dealing in "real" property that is fixed and cannot be removed, they have extra security. This is often false, as what they are accepting in fact are some pieces of paper, not the real property itself.

NOTES

1. *A Compendium of Bunk*, Carey and Sherman, Charles C. Thomas, 1976, pp. 73-79.
2. *Big Time Operator's Manual*, Scot Tinker, Eden Press, 1977, p. 34.

3. Ibid., pp. 26-27.

4. Ibid., pp. 28-31.

5. *A Compendium of Bunk*, p. 74.

6. *Big Time Operator's Manual*, pp. 32-33.

7. *Professional Con Games, Schemes, and Frauds*, Carl Dorski, Roadrunner Publications, 1979, pp. 3-4.

8. *Big Time Operator's Manual*, p. 9.

9. *Clipping The Flocks*, Scot Tinker, Eden Press, p. 25.

10. *Short Cons*, Scot Tinker, Eden Press, pp. 30-31.

11. *A Compendium of Bunk*, p. 71.

STOCK MARKET FRAUDS

It might be accurate to say the whole market is a fraud, and indeed some people think so. The stock market, like the insurance business, is an example of a legitimate effort evolving into widespread fraud.

Let's take a quick view at how the market operates to understand the opportunities for fraud. The stock market is set up as a clearing house for the buying and selling of stock. Anyone who wants to buy and sell stock must do it through a broker, who collects his commission on the value of the stock he handles for his clients.

The values of stocks go up and down. An issue of stock may go up if the company wins a lucrative contract. It may go down if its sales are down. Rumors that concern a company may also affect the price of its stock. Trading in the stock, even if there is no apparent reason for the activity, will affect the price.

With this basic groundwork, we can see the opportunities for fraud. Firstly, we have the broker. He does not collect if his client's stock goes up or down, but only if the client buys or sells. He understands the more he can persuade his client to trade, the more commissions he will earn. Investors try to earn money on the stock market by buying a stock when the price is low and selling when it goes up. They sometimes seek advice from brokers, and it's a rare occasion when a broker will tell his client to stand pat, not to buy or sell anything. The broker always has a stock issue to push, something which "looks good" or "promising," and the broker is always assured of his commission, even if the client loses his shirt.

Brokers always try to stimulate sales, for that is the only way they can earn commissions. Some of them, even the big-name ones, operate "boiler-rooms," telephone sales operations in which their agents telephone people to try to persuade them to buy stocks. Those who bite are led on by dreams of riches from trading stocks, which the brokers avidly encourage. Clients may also be affected by the influence of the various books that appear with titles that follow the pattern *How I Made A Zillion Dollars In The*

Stock Market. These authors tell the same story: how they started out with very little money and, by their genius, parlayed the small sum into great wealth. They usually don't mention luck, preferring to take the entire credit themselves. Of course, the people who lose don't write books, as a title of *How I Lost My Shirt In The Stock Market* would not sell well.

Some brokers and investors make their own luck. They know hype and chain reactions affect the price of stocks, and they will quietly buy a stock when it is low, then plant something in the rumor mill. In doing this, they can exploit innocent clients by telling them the rumor they're planting, and in effect, using the client's money to "churn" the market, to stimulate activity. It usually happens that the price of a quiescent stock will go up as the volume of trading in it increases. This is called the "chain reaction." Brokers and investors out to "make a killing" will start the chain reaction by trading with each other. Others, attracted by the activity, will buy this stock, even though they don't understand exactly why there is such interest in this issue.

Some operators, who may be stockbrokers or executives of companies whose stock is on the market, try to profit by using "inside information," such as quietly buying an issue knowing that the price will rise when a forthcoming contract is announced. This is illegal, but people do it anyway. It is difficult for the Securities and Exchange Commission to prosecute if the operator covers his tracks even slightly, and a simple way to do this is to have a mutual aid agreement with another person. The operator tips off the accomplice when and what to buy, and the transaction does not have his name on it. It is easy to arrange a way of splitting the profits later. If the accomplice is an executive of another company, they can reciprocate favors such as these, making the arrangement untraceable, as there will be no suspicious transaction in the name of the one who has access to the "inside" information.

"Penny Stocks" are perhaps more popular now than ever. These are stocks in relatively small and little known companies, their prices rarely being over a dollar a share, which makes them affordable to working-class people. While investment in *any* stock is risky, because we don't know what the future will bring, buying penny stocks is *very* risky, as the companies involved are new, have no "track record," and the management may or may not be able to do the job. However, stockbrokers don't really care about the future prospects of a particular stock. They seek to earn commissions now, in the present, and some operate "boiler rooms" to push penny stocks with people who have never played the market before.[1] It's important to note that, although many of the penny stocks are those of real and legitimate, though struggling, companies, some of them are outright frauds. Some dishonest operators, not satisfied with the profits they can make through conventional stock market manipulations, seek to make a killing by buying a defunct corporation, using it as a shell, and promoting its stock. By setting up a boiler room operation, the operator can keep both the commission and the price of the stock.[2]

Sometimes, the stockbroker is the victim of a fraud. One way is for the fraud artist to place an order for the purchase of stock by phone. It sometimes happens that the broker, especially if it's a busy day, will not check if the "customer" has an account. What happens next depends on whether the stock goes up or down. If it goes up, the "customer" shows up to pay for it, and then resells it at a profit. If it goes down, the "customer" does not show up, and the broker is stuck.[3]

Some overtly fraudulent investments are not offered on the stock market. Sometimes, the fraud artist will approach victims who obviously are wealthy, in a setting such as a yacht or country club, and by subtle play-acting, entice them into an "investment" in a new invention, design, or product. At times, the preparations for the scam can be very elaborate, and the fraud artist can string his victims along through several stages. Typically, the fraud artist, once he gets the initial investment, will wait awhile before asking for more money. He knows it is easier to wring money from someone by steps instead of in one big bite. The con man will announce there is a need for more money to provide "working capital," pay "expenses," etc. Sometimes he'll be so brazen as to sell stock certificates, which may be those of a shell, or dummy corporation, or may be overt forgeries.[4] It is easy to forge stock certificates, and some swindlers have them printed by legitimate **printers and use the phoney certificates as collateral.**

Commodities are not stocks, but the commodities market works approximately the same way as the stock market. The brokers, earning commissions, try to persuade as many people as they can to trade as much as they can in the commodities they handle.

It gets to be really dangerous when the individual buyer does not buy a commodity outright, but gets involved in agreements to buy at a later date, called a "future." Sometimes, he'll buy an "option," which can get him into more trouble. The salesmen who push "options" and "futures" carefully gloss over the fact that the buyer is not buying real goods when he hands over his money, but simply pieces of paper. The one who falls for this "pitch" can find himself seriously hurt, and without recourse.

NOTES

1. *Big Time Operator's Manual,* Scot Tinker, Eden Press, 1977, p. 20.

2. Ibid., p. 21.

3. Ibid., p. 17.

4. *A Compendium of Bunk,* Carey and Sherman, Charles C. Thomas, 1976, pp. 107-114.

TANGENTIAL CONS

Tangential cons are deceptions not for immediate and direct gains, but as preparations for later criminal acts. A good example, used every day, is "casing the joint" by posing as a customer or salesman.[1]

Eugene Villiod, French detective, says "opportunity makes the thief." He also correctly points out that some thieves make their own opportunities. In real life, only the most raw and inexperienced thief commits his crime on impulse, without first carrying out a reconnaissance. Depending on the type of crime, the reconnaissance can be crude or sophisticated.

A solitary robber may just need basic information, such as the location of the cash register, the number of staff behind the counter, opening and closing hours, and the presence of any countermeasures, such as an alarm system. A burglar will be more interested in whether there is alarm tape on the windows, magnetic or induction alarms on the doors, the location of the control box, and whether the alarm rings a gong outside the store or a "silent alarm" that sends a signal to the police station or security service without alerting the intruder. Acting upon this information, he'll plan to muffle the gong if there is one, or to cut the wires if it's a silent alarm. Both robbers and burglars will want to "case" the surroundings, to plan getaway routes and note the frequency of police patrols.

There is little the store owner can do about this. He can't refuse admission to his store, although in some unusually rough **neighborhoods, liquour stores are barred and sell only through a teller's grill.**

Better organized burglars and robbers use an advance man, a specialist who does not participate in the act itself but who seeks out and presents information about the target. He may also be a planner, devising the mode of entry and the subsequent events. For this service, he gets a share of the "take."

Advance men are specialists, not strong-arm men, and they develop special skills to supplement their eyes, ears, and common sense. They are, in a sense, con men, because often they play a role as they gain access. The advance man may pose as a salesman, inspector, or service technician in order to scout the premises.

Sometimes he's not playing a role, but really is such a person. A minority of such mobile people, with criminal contacts, know they can earn extra money with no risk by passing on "tips" about likely targets to the right people.

There is no defense against this type of scout. He is the person he claims to be, and checking with his employer will verify this. The typewriter repairman or telephone installer comes onto the premises with the express permission of the person who ordered the service, and his cover is unbreakable.

The complex technology of the Twentieth Century has not only increased the number of crimes, but has made carrying them out successfully easier for the criminal. The same telephone that permits a citizen to report a crime promptly to the police enables the burglar to check if anyone is home before he approaches. The increased affluence which has more people than before living in one-family houses on fenced-off lots for privacy permits the burglar to work unobserved by neighbors.

House and apartment dwellers are also targets for criminals. The advance man can be a salesman, bogus or legitimate, who under the guise of selling his product or service often gains admission to the home, where he can scout for items of unusual value that would make an attempt worthwhile. In conversation with the resident, he can elicit information that is valuable to a burglar. On the pretext of visiting the bathroom, he can scout another room or two. One who poses as an "inspector" can have the run of the house.

Burglars, although sometimes armed and dangerous, usually don't want to run into anyone when they're doing a "job." They want to know when the residents will be away from home. As a last minute check, they'll phone the target. If nobody answers, they know the resident is either out or in the bathroom. An unlisted number is not necessarily protection, as the advance man may have had the opportunity to read the number from the phone while in the home.

As a final check, the burglar will scout the premises before his final approach, checking if there is a car in the driveway or garage, or if there is noise coming from the home. The final step is to ring the bell. If, after several rings, nobody answers, he'll know the "coast is clear." If someone does come to the door, he'll pose as someone who rang the wrong bell, or if the hour is appropriate, a salesman. The stereotype of the criminal with a mask and a blackjack sticking out of his pocket will not fit him.

Telephone "surveys" can be subterfuges for tangential cons. One example is the car-theft-to-order ring. In states in which motor vehicle registrations are not accessible to the public, the scout for the ring has the choice of riding the streets until he sees a car in demand, or phoning until he finds one. He'll pretend to be making a survey on car care, asking questions about the maintenance the car has received, and of course the make and model. For his select customers, he'll want a "clean" car, one that has been well-treated, and he'll want to know where to find it at his convenience. Riding the streets means he strikes at targets of opportunity, forced to steal them where he finds them. While there are car thieves who use inertia hammers to rip out the door lock, the high-class "car-to-order" thief does not want to damage the car, and prefers to make off with it at his leisure.

An unusual method of "setting up" a victim for a robbery involves a large cash payment. When this criminal wants a new car, he buys it for cash, bringing the money to the sales office but first tipping off his partner. As soon as the buyer pays for the car, a perfectly legitimate transaction, the buyer leaves and his partner drops in to rob the dealer. They later split the money.[2]

NOTES

1. *Crooks, Con Men, and Cheats,* Eugene Villiod, Gambler's Book Club Press, 1980, pp. 88-98.
2. *Professional Con Games, Schemes, and Frauds,* Carl Dorski, Roadrunner Press, 1980, pp. 22-23.

TECHNOLOGICAL FRAUD

Certain aspects of high-tech fraud would require a book of their own, but we won't concern ourselves with the intricacies of computer crime and other massive complexities because most of us won't even get close to them. There are some ways in which cheats and con men do use bank computers to defraud others, and we'll look at one of those ways now:

A plastic, magnetically-imprinted bank card, designed for electronic banking, can be used as an adjunct to a fraud. In most systems, a deposit at an electronic teller will show immediately in the balance on the printed slip, although the money won't be credited to the account until a human teller can open the deposit envelope and verify the amount. The cards can also call up a statement of the account balance, even without a deposit. This weakness can make it easy for a con man.

The swindler, determined to take advantage of this situation, goes to the electronic teller after the bank's closing, and makes a "deposit" of a large sum. The envelope he puts into the slot is empty, however, but this does not register with the computer. This is the key to getting away with a piece of merchandise and leaving only a small deposit. If the item in question is a car, for example, the fraud artist can take the seller to the electronic teller and show him the balance in his account of fifty thousand dollars, as proof of ability to pay. If, as the smart con man will arrange, the meeting takes place after banking hours, there is no way the victim can determine he's being set up. The fraud artist makes off with the car, and the victim waits and waits and waits.

Anyone who carries a plastic card, whether it be for banking or straight credit card, should be aware that some thieves specialize in stealing and fencing these precious pieces of plastic. Similarly, a businessman who deals with the public should be aware of the procedures for handling the threat of stolen, expired, or forged credit cards. Some credit card artists can evade being traced because they know that, until the "hot list" of lost and stolen cards comes out, the merchant is not required to check with the company unless the amount of the purchase exceeds a certain amount.[1]

The limits on credit card fraud are sky-high. A swindler using a stolen or lost credit card, can even charge amounts over the limit, as when stopping at a hotel. The hotel won't verify the amount until the final bill is settled, and the swindler can quietly leave long before then.[2]

The swindler who is in collusion either with the legitimate "owner" of a plastic card or with a dishonest merchant can, by simple falsification, take in a lot of money or goods in a very short time. The partner simply hands over his credit card to the swindler, delays notifying the home company, and meanwhile the fraud artist uses the card profusely, secure in the knowledge that he's in no danger of even being challenged for forty-eight hours. At the end of that period, the partner reports his card "lost," knowing the law makes him liable for only the first fifty dollars.[3]

A small-time rip-off, more common now that most deposit slips are magnetically imprinted, is for a fraud artist to open up a checking account, or an electronic savings account as a first step. It's vital for him to have a means of withdrawing money from this account without showing his face in a bank office, for the risk of detection is great enough to make this very dangerous.

The second step is to have many duplicate slips printed, without a name but with the magnetic number on the bottom. The fraud artist then goes around to several bank branches and places these slips in the compartments at the customer service tables.

Inevitably, some customers will notice the discrepancy. Also, inevitably, some will not, and the swindler who keeps his plastic card handy to make withdrawals as the money flows in and before the account is stopped can collect these intentionally misplaced deposits.

Turning to another currently popular type of fraud involving a computer, we find the "computer-dating" services. These are just variations on the old lonely-hearts clubs, but with a modern twist that is real at times and outright false at others. The program works in this manner:

The operator sends each applicant a "computer form" containing a large number of questions, some very personal. Allegedly, the answers will be "analyzed" by a computer to determine the personality type, and the applicant will be matched by the computer to the most compatible personality in its memory bank.

There are several things wrong with this basic idea. One is that matchmaking is not a science, but an art, and there are no scientifically valid criteria for matching people by computer. Even if the test handed to the applicant is designed by a "psychologist," and even if the "psychologist" is real, the test is not validated through the use of control groups comprising thousands of testees, an essential before a test can be considered valid.

Another trouble area is the way the "computer dating service" is presented to the applicant. The operator promises the applicant that he or she will be matched with intelligent, attractive members of the opposite sex. According to the operator, only the best people, upwardly mobile and very well-off and sexy, form the dating pool. The people who are taken in by such operators perhaps do not stop to think it out, and do not realize that the truly superior group of people described in the brochure does not need a computer or any other kind of dating service, that they have no trouble finding dates on their own.[4]

More than any other, this is an unfinished chapter. Technological improvements bring new frauds into the realm of possibility constantly, and new techniques of access and communication bring with them new versions of fast-moving fraud.

NOTES

1. *The Fraud Report,* 1977, Financial Management Associates, 3824 East Indian School Road, Phoenix, AZ 85018 Section 2, p. 5.

2. Ibid., Section 2, p. 7.

3. Ibid., Section 2, p. 8.

4. *A Compendium of Bunk,* Carey and Sherman, 1976, Charles C. Thomas.

TELEPHONE GAMES

The telephone is a modern convenience, but it would be only a minor exaggeration to call it an instrument of evil, in some situations. There are many frauds that depend on the telephone for success.

We start with the classic and simple fraud, whereby an individual using a pay phone gets a free call. The person inserts a coin and dials "Operator." When the operator answers, the game goes like this:

"Operator, I was trying to get my number, 123-4567, and I heard a couple of clicks and the line went dead. I lost my coin."

"I'm sorry. I'll try it for you. Give me your address and we'll send you your coin back in the mail."

Another game to play with pay phones is to tape record the sound of coins dropping, using a small and portable machine. When calling long distance, playing the tape for the operator will fool her into thinking that there are actually coins deposited.[1]

There is a category of people called "phone phreaks," who circumvent the phone company's safeguards because they are talented in electronics and construct devices to fake control tones that switch long-distance lines, or even by having them billed to another party. In some instances, the phone phreaks are able to break into supposedly secure lines belonging to the government and route their calls through them.

Annoying as these people may be to the telephone company, we can't get very indignant about their actions because firstly, they're more fun and games than victimization. Secondly, it is hard to get excited over a corporate giant, such as the phone company, losing nickels and dimes to individuals.

It's another matter when criminals use the telephone to victimize the innocent. We can recognize the distinction, although the phone company pretends that it does not exist, and treats con artists just as it does other customers. This practice seems bizarre when compared to that of the Postal Service.

The Postal Service keeps a staff of Postal Inspectors who investigate mail fraud. By contrast, the phone company, another medium used by fraud artists, uses its security operatives mainly to oversee the security of its physical facilities and to pursue clients who don't pay their bills. This is why, although mail fraud is big business, telephone fraud is gigantic.

The classic example of telephone fraud is the "boiler room." This is a room full of desks, phones, and people who run down lists generally taken from the telephone directory and pitch the people who answer. Sometimes the boiler roon is legitimate, as in selling tickets to the fireman's ball. More often, there will be an element of deception. One pitch went like this:

"Hello, Mr. Smith. This is Mr. Jones from the Brooklyn Children's Shelter. In cooperation with the Daily Pitch, we're asking people to help the Brooklyn Shelter. If you subscribe to the Pitch the Shelter will get full credit for that, and you'll be helping needy kids."

In reality, this was just a device to sell newspaper subscriptions, and the "Shelter" got, instead of "full credit," a donation of 25 cents for each subscription.[2]

Phoney charities are classic devices for conning people out of their hard-earned money, and they work on the phone as well as they do face to face. They lend themselves well to boiler room operations, because the con man can hire innocent people to make the pitches for him. Not having polished and professional salesmen make the sales talks is not a handicap in charity frauds, because sales "pros" would be out of place in such a setting.

For products and services not claiming to be charitable, the pitches can be ingenious indeed, and the telephone techniques literally far-reaching. Boiler rooms, like legitimate businesses, use WATS lines to obtain low-cost direct dialing across the country. A crew working in New York can canvass the country systematically. A recent development is the computerized telephone dialer, which dials one number after another until there is an answer, then plays a taped sales message to whoever is listening, and signals a human salesman if the person is still on the line after the end of the message. This device saves a lot of salesmen's time, and wastes a lot of other people's.

Sometimes the victim has a chance of recognizing the fraud because the approach follows well-known patterns. A voice on the telephone which announces that it is making a "survey" is usually the beginning of a sales pitch. A caller who tells his victim that he wants to give him a "free gift" is also trying to sell something. Sometimes there will be a "quiz," with an easily answered question that then "qualifies" the victim for the "prize" or special "low introductory offer." Some of the varied approaches used are truly ingenious.[3]

A particularly brazen fraud, operated out of a phone booth, was the "Cadillac" game used by a man who passed himself off as the producer of a famous television show. He'd ask the victim to appear on the show, and added that part of the fee for the appearance would be a Cadillac. He told the victim that a representative would be in touch to help them select the car.

Several days later, a man with the proper credentials would show up, and tell the victim that of course, all expenses would be paid for the appearance on the show, and that he could select his Cadillac right away from some brochures. If necessary, they'd go to the local Cadillac agency, where the victim could examine the cars before making his selection, which would be ordered through the television production company, not the local dealer.

The "representative" would then carefully tell the victim that, while the producer could legally give away the prize, the law required that the sales tax and license fee be paid by the person receiving it. He'd extract the amount from the victim, who would never see him again.[4]

Answering the phone nowadays can be a hazard, not so much to the health but to the wallet. The use of the phone for sales pitches and for fraud is now so great that some people think of it as "pollution."

NOTES

1. *Professional Con Games, Schemes, and Frauds,* Carl Dorski, Roadrunner Publications, 1979, p. 27.

2. Personal knowledge of the author.

3. *A Compendium of Bunk,* Carey and Sherman, Charles C. Thomas, 1976, pp. 46-47.

4. *The Fraud Report,* 1977, Financial Management Associates. Section 5, pp. 11-13.

THIRD-PARTY CONTRACTS

An interesting opportunity for the fraud artist, and a great danger to the consumer, is the "third-party" contract. This means that when a customer buys an article on credit, the credit being supplied by a party not connected with the seller, the lender is not responsible for the quality of the item and has the right to demand payment.

While the law in this regard varies from state to state, and some states have certain consumer protection laws that affect third-party contracts, the procedure is usually the same. The customer buys an item on credit, using a credit card, securing a loan from a finance company, or a mortgage from a bank. He is then obligated to make payments, regardless of the conditions of the sale or the item purchased. Any questions regarding the quality of the goods or the terms of the sales contract do not involve the creditor, and are strictly between the seller and the buyer.

Third-party contracts are daily occurrences, and often do not pose any problem at all. It's also important to note that when there is a problem, it is often possible to resolve it without concern over the terms of payment.

When a customer buys an article from a reputable outlet, and pays for it with a bank credit card, not a store charge account card, he's obligated to pay the amount due. When there is a problem with defective merchandise, the reputable outlet will either repair or replace the item, or will take it back and issue a credit memo, cancelling the original amount charged to the credit card.

The interesting opportunity for the fraud artist is that in selling a large-ticket item, he can obtain his money quickly, with the customer footing the bill for the finance charges, and in fact if the seller acts as an agent for the credit company, processing the paperwork, he often earns a small commission from the lender on top of his profit.

With the money in his pocket, the fraud artist can leave town. The defrauded customer is left "holding the bag," obligated to make the time payments. In the cases of fraud artists who stay at the same location for years (used car lots are good examples) the fraud artist knows that the customer has, through the credit source, already paid him and cannot hold out payment to enforce his demand for satisfaction.

The danger for the customer is obvious. As we've seen, he's left holding the bag, and often has no recourse. While he is also left holding the bag in small transactions, the amount of money lost is not as painful. Being obligated to make payments on a car that doesn't run, however, will often prevent him from getting credit to finance one that does, and if he needs a car for daily use, he'll be in deep trouble.

In the case of a fraud artist who has left town, the effects are often more far-reaching. Not only is pursuit and apprehension of the fraud artist more difficult, but the customer may be left to deal with a contract upon which the vendor has defaulted. An example is when the customer buys an appliance, such as a sewing machine or water softener, and the transaction includes either a warranty or a service and maintenance contract. Although the customer will not get the service called for in the contract, he must continue to make the payments.

What we can learn from this is clear: Apart from the extra thought that must accompany any purchase which involves a large amount of money, the customer must also be wary of any that call for third-party contracts because of the danger of that extra degree of victimization. Except for states which have provisions in their consumer-protection laws that cover third-party contracts, the defrauded customer has no recourse.

STRIKING BACK IS HEALTHY

In recent years there's been much attention paid to the plight of the criminal, and in the process the victim has been forgotten. It's easy to overlook the fact that the victim loses in two ways, materially and psychologically.

Whatever the nature of the crime, police and psychologists have observed victims undergoing a psychological upheaval that, in some instances, can be very severe. If the crime is violent, there is mental as well as physical trauma. Even in the absence of severe physical injury the victim suffers the after-effects of anxiety and fear. In many cases, there is a feeling of helplessness, which is the beginning of depression.

The victim of fraud has a mental burden to bear, although he almost never has to cope with violence or even the threat of violence. Yet, he has lost, and the circumstances of his loss make it more depressing. The victim of a burglary may be very unhappy at the loss, but the thief, operating by stealth, is contemptible. The fraud victim has to live with the knowledge that he's been outwitted. The fraud victim, strangely also, does not get the sympathy from friends and family that other victims do. Even the victim of rape will find sympathetic faces, people who understand that it might have happened to them.

The fraud victim has no such support. He may quite rightly feel that the attitude of others is: "He let himself in for it, the jerk." This is a blow to the ego, and intensifies the victim's problem.

We've seen that, in crimes of violence, the law is clearcut and the police will make an effort, although the clearance rate for crimes is discouragingly low, and the net result is that only one or two percent of criminals go to prison. In cases of fraud, the police may not even recognize that there's been a crime committed, telling the victim: "It's a civil matter." This leaves the victim high and dry, not even knowing where he stands.

In all crimes, punishment of the criminal is psychologically satisfying to the victim. If it is direct and personal retribution, it satisfies the need to hurt the criminal as badly as the victim was hurt. If it is retribution by the state, at least there is the satisfaction that justice will prevail, that it is a well-ordered world in which the bad guys are punished.

When, as so often happens, the criminal is not caught and punished, it leaves the victim angry and frustrated. He's justifiably angry at the wrong that was done to him, and he's frustrated by a system that doesn't seem to work. Reading of the many other cases in which criminals get away with it reinforces and intensifies the feeling of helplessness.

This section is aimed at the victim and potential victim, in an effort to help both in protective means and the means of striking back. It's mentally healthy to be able to protect oneself. It's mentally healthy to want to strike back after being hurt.

We'll consider three areas: passive defense, in which we look at simple methods that are very effective for the time and effort involved, active defense, and counter-attack.

PASSIVE DEFENSE

Passive defense consists of measures you can take, without much effort and at no cost, to reduce your vulnerability to fraud. The principles are well-known, and the major disagreement is on how far to go.

Keeping a low profile is an obvious first step. This means blending in with the crowd and not standing out as a potential target for a fraud artist. Keeping a low profile also means not flashing a roll of money, not dressing exceptionally opulently, not having an obviously expensive brand of luggage when you travel, and perhaps even making it a point not to travel first class. Custom license plates, like expensive cars, are out. If you look prosperous enough, someone might think you're worth kidnapping.

Awareness of the basic frauds and some of the modern variations is the next step. Learn to recognize the basic con games and know the roles that con men and their accomplices play. It is impossible to keep up with all of the new wrinkles in fraud, partly because no true encyclopedia of fraud exists, and it's hard to see how anyone could compile one without its becoming obsolete before it got into print. Still, you don't need to know it all, just enough so you'll be aware of the scams that someone might pull on you.

While some authorities advise being withdrawn and not talking to strangers,[1] carrying out all of their recommendations would result in a totally closed-in lifestyle. It is not necessary to go that far. It is important not to be too free and easy with strangers, and to pick your associates carefully. Being aware of the fact that "sheet writers" and fake bail bondsmen frequent conventions and vacation resorts, it is prudent to be wary about discussing personal affairs with recent acquaintances. It's not necessary to distrust all strangers and treat them with suspicion and coldness bordering on hostility. You need only to be aware that seemingly harmless details you may divulge about yourself can be used against you by a fraud artist.

Gambling with strangers is a no-no. The floating crap game or the "friendly" game of poker in a hotel room that suddenly turns ugly are two prospects that are easy to avoid.

Lending money to strangers is in one sense the same as lending it to a friend. It boils down to the question, "How much can you afford to lose?" Most of us have been "stiffed" by a friend who simply "forgot" to pay back a small loan. With a stranger, no matter what the story, we have no way of knowing at the outset whether the borrower is for real or just another slick deceiver. A decision we can make in advance, and which will cover all circumstances is the amount we're willing to lend. We must be prepared for the possibility that our humanitarian impulses will lead us into trouble, and be prepared to cut our losses.

Another aspect of passive defense also has to do with mental preparation. It's important to develop a certain skepticism and to understand that if an offer sounds "too good to be true," it probably is. There really is little chance of getting "something for nothing," or "striking it rich." Even if there were, why would a stranger share his newly-found secret of wealth with you? Because you're a nice guy? There are adults who succumb to the charming, smiling stranger who's going to make them wealthy, although if you were to ask these adults if they believe in the tooth fairy, they'd feel insulted.

Some of the precautions you can take serve double-duty. Not widely spreading the news of your impending travel not only forestalls some of the away-from-home schemes, but also helps to avoid being burglarized while away.

Some precautions present problems. Not having your name and address on the outside of your luggage helps to prevent some swindles, but it also prevents or impedes its return if lost. Having identification on the inside only is largely futile, as a baggage thief will surely open the case.

While it's going too far to distrust all strangers, there are some cases in which precautions are prudent. Picking up hitch-hikers is not dangerous most of the time, but there's always the occasional one who'll make you wish you'd never seen him. Each person has to assess the risk for himself.

Never letting a stranger into the home is another yes-no-maybe situation. While it's obvious that taking a hitch-hiker home with you, no matter how nice he seems or how sorry his tale of woe, is often the prelude to trouble, it's impossible to generalize more than that. The person who knocks at your door and asks to use the phone may be a criminal or someone in trouble, and it's not always possible to follow the conventional wisdom and make him or her wait outside while you place the call for them. In bad weather, few people can resist letting in a stranger who claims that his car stalled.

There are, of course, repairman and "inspector" types who want to get into your home, and checking credentials and verifying identities with their central office is a wise precaution. In any event, you will know whether or not you sent for a repairman.

In doubtful situations, try to pay by check, as many a con man will find a check a problem if he's seeking just quick cash. A check also gives you the opportunity to stop payment if, after checking or thinking it over, you decide you're in for a fraud. In any situation with someone asking you for money, unless it's a transaction you've initiated, be careful. Accepting a C.O.D. parcel, paying off someone's debt, buying a subscription or putting a down payment on a piece of property are ways some frauds start.

Finally, if you're one of the millions of Americans who may let him or herself into a sexually compromising situation, be very careful, not only of your partner, but of the situation as a whole. The care you need to take depends on your situation and your habits. If you're a husband seeking some fun on the side at a convention away from home, and you have an understanding wife, your situation is not as acute as that of the homosexual who works as a schoolteacher and who picks up young male prostitutes in the park.

Anyone with sexual habits that are either illegal or which may cause embarrassment if discovered must learn great discretion. As with other threats, there is no perfect defense, and the sexually deviant person will always be at least minimally exposed to risk.

SOURCES

1. *Complete Security Handbook,* Anthony B. Herbert, 1983, **MacMillan Publishing Co., Inc., 866 Third Avenue, New York, NY 10022.**
This book covers all aspects of personal security, but the precautions listed, if followed as closely as the author suggests, lead to a very restricted and fearful lifestyle that few people would willingly adopt. Most of us are willing to accept a slightly higher risk for more freedom.

THE ROLE OF THE POLICE

There are two main reasons fraud artists have such success:

1. Public attitudes. Most people tend to think of crime as they see it on TV: shootouts, car chases, and unrelenting violence practiced by desperate or psychopathic criminals. The news media help this image of violent crime, faithfully reporting every rape and murder, giving the bulk of front-page space to the criminal who kidnaps and murders a baby, not the smooth-talking fraud artist. The public remains unaware of the greater volume of "white collar" crime, and being unaware, is more open to exploitation.

2. Police attitudes. The police feel most comfortable with a straightforward violent crime, one in which there is no need to deal with such intangibles as pattern and intent. They are geared to overwhelm violence with superior force, and this shows even in their equipment. Police officers carry revolvers, but few have even a pocket calculator as part of their equipment. Some of the larger departments have a fraud or "bunco" squad as part of their detective bureaus, but numerically they are few, although non-violent crimes far outnumber the violent ones, and are more profitable.

The police are wary of entering the field of civil disputes. It has happened many times that citizens and businessmen have tried to use the police as a collection agency to collect money due them. Police know they do not belong in matters that properly belong in civil, not criminal, court. In many instances, they do not even recognize a fraud scheme as being one.

The attitudes on the parts of both the police and the public form a combination that greatly lubricates the way for the fraud artist. When a citizen does make a complaint (and many do not) the police reaction is likely to be: "That's a civil matter." Often, it is not clear to the police that an incident forms part of a pattern, unless several victims report the incidents.[1]

Allied to this is the difficulty of convincing some people they're letting themselves be victimized. For example, there was an incident of a woman who phoned the fraud squad regarding a chain letter she'd received. The detective who spoke to her spent some time explaining that chain letters are money-making schemes only for the ones who start the chains, and her chances of becoming rich were nil. He added that participating in a chain letter was a misdemeanor, but she remained unconvinced.[2]

Reporting the incident to the police often is not enough to bring the affair to a successful conclusion. To obtain a prosecution and conviction, it may be necessary for the victim to take the time to testify in court. If you've been victimized, you may find this difficult, for several reasons:

1. The place where you're required to testify may be quite far from your home, as many con games victimize people who are away from home on vacation or at a convention. Sheet writers and **phoney bail bondsmen, for example, do this.**

2. You may feel the effort required is not worth it. If you've lost only one hundred dollars, for example, and you have to take a lot of time off from work to testify, the effort would be out of proportion.

3. Coming out into the open may be personally embarrassing for you. If you've been a victim of the badger game, for example, reporting the incident will mean that you have to face the publicity, and the more serious your role the more harm this can do to you. Many victims, such as homosexuals and married men, feel they can't take the heat. Fraud artists count on this and it often happens the police will know of the operations of a fraud artist, but won't be able to find any people willing to cooperate in the prosecution.

4. Conviction rates are low. Part of the reason is, in many states a technicality of the law prevents the prosecutor from mentioning the defendant's criminal record to the jury, although the judge will know of it and take it into account in sentencing. The reason for this wrinkle in the law is that knowledge of a prior conviction may prejudice the jury in considering guilt or innocence in the current case. While this may be valid for other types of crimes, it is counter-productive in fraud cases, where there is so much deception involved and where an important part of the case is the

pattern. It's easy for the fraud artist to convince a jury that "it was just a misunderstanding," in one instance, but if there is a long record of such "misunderstandings," he will find it much harder to persuade the jury to believe him.

5. If you're the victim of fraud, you may decide the police will not be as helpful as they would be in other types of crimes. Hard reality is much different from the illusions some people carry. The real police, unlike TV cops, do not always get their man, and the picture becomes even more discouraging when they don't seem to be making even a reasonable effort. For example, in some cities, the police will not send an officer to investigate a burglary, instead taking the report by telephone.

There is one exception to the disappointing performance of the authorities. The victim of fraud can retaliate by sending the "Gestapo" after the fraud artist. Some Americans refer to the Internal Revenue Service as the "Gestapo," and there is a certain resemblance in one respect: both are terribly efficient. The original Gestapo derived its frightening reputation not so much because of brutish sadists who beat the arrestees mercilessly, but because Gestapo officers were mostly brilliant men who were good at their jobs. The Internal Revenue Service, despite much bad publicity, is staffed largely by dedicated people, and in the case of a fraud artist, you can put them to work for you.[3]

The IRS has a program of rewarding informers, sometimes called the "Turn in a friend" program, in which it pays cash rewards (taxable, of course) to people who tip them off to those who are evading income taxes. Unlike local police, the IRS is a nationwide agency, and has formidable investigative resources. Also, the IRS will devote a great deal of manpower and effort to getting a conviction, mainly to make examples of tax cheats and show others they can't get away with it.

If you have reason to believe the person who defrauded you is not declaring his income, and if you can pinpoint him to the IRS, you can give them a "tip" which will start an investigation. The IRS will pick up the ball and you probably won't have to testify in court, as the prosecution will be for evading taxes, not victimizing a specific person. You could even make some money from the affair, which may or may not pay you back for what you've lost.

NOTES

1. *Fraud Investigation,* Glick and Newsome, Charles C. Thomas, 1974, p. 11.

2. *A Compendium of Bunk,* Carey and Sherman, 1976, Charles C. Thomas, pp. 7-8.

3. Ibid., pp. 91-92.

ACTIVE DEFENSE

Active defense is just that — active, direct means of defending yourself against a fraud artist, but stopping short of serious retaliation. Although in principle the distinction between defense and counter-attack should be very clear, in real life it is blurred, and there's an element of counter-attack in some defensive measures.

Let's start with the mail. Each day brings its quota of junk mail, with the fabulous free offers and announcements that you've just won a contest. Often, these littering letters have business reply cards or envelopes included. Instead of throwing them all away, seal and mail them. The recipient will have to pay the collect postage on each one.

Moving on to the phone, it's a good idea to ask who's calling each time the phone rings. Instead of allowing a salesperson to waste several minutes of your time with a "survey" or other nonsense, ask immediately for the name and company affiliation. Don't be shy. If the offer is for a "free gift," tell the person to send it in the mail, that it's not necessary for you to be at home to receive a gift. That usually stops them cold. If there's only a taped message on the other end of the line, you'll know and be able to hang up.

A telephone answering machine is a good way of screening out junk calls. Most salespeople will simply hang up when a robot answers them, not wishing to waste their time. Keeping the machine on, even when home, and using the "monitor" function will save you the need to answer calls you don't want.

A simple tactic is to hang up, without warning and without saying "goodby." You'll find it easier to ignore your impulse to be polite after the salespeople have interrupted your supper for the fourteenth evening in a row, and you'll find it hard not to hang up with an obscenity.

The essence of good tactics in active defense is simplicity. There's no need for complicated plans, which sometimes are more trouble than they're worth.

Coping with panhandlers, whatever their come-on, is simple. Tell the panhandler you left your wallet home that day. This will work especially well on the office panhandler who comes around with his tale of having lost his wallet and the contents of his briefcase.

The quickest way of coping with the "pigeon drop" and similar scams is to suggest that the best thing to do with the "lost" item is to turn it in to the police. You'll be surprised how quickly he'll lose interest in you.

The simplest turn-off for any money game, hot goods scam, or any scheme to extract money from you on the spot is to say that you don't have enough money with you. If the con man wants twenty dollars from you, tell him you only have twenty cents. If the con man suggests that you go to your bank to withdraw the amount, tell him that your bankbook or plastic card is at your lawyer's , as there was a problem that needed straightening out.

Looking at the simplest methods, always get up to go to the kitchen or bathroom when you're watching TV and the commercials come on. They're all lies, anyway. Why waste time watching even for a minute?

Learn to use time to your advantage. As we've seen, the majority of con men are hit-and-run artists, straining to make a quick buck and leave town. They'll try to "hustle" you, to press you to act immediately. The best thing you can do, if something seems not quite right, is to temporize. Playing for time will work in almost any situation. To select an extreme and ridiculous example, if you're a witness to the "flop" game, in which a "doctor" takes up a collection for an undernourished person laying on the sidewalk, it's easy to say: "I left my wallet home. Give me your card and I'll send you a check."

Using your lawyer, whether you really have one or not, will save you a lot of grief and give you an impregnable position from which to resist high-pressure tactics. Whether the deal is a car or a piece of real estate, if you think something's wrong, dig in your heels and say flatly: "I never sign a contract without showing it to my lawyer." If you're fifty miles out in the boonies, looking at worthless land, the same isolation the con artists see working for them will work for you, if you insist you always show legal papers to your lawyer before signing. At least, this tactic enables you to play for time. If the deal is valid, it will surely still be there tommorrow. If the salesman insists this is a once-in-a-lifetime opportunity, that's almost a sure tip-off it's a fraud.

Knowing your prices is basically passive defense, but using the information actively is another matter. Door-to-door sales people will often try to sell you something at an exorbitant price. In principle, the salesman should never have gotten in the door, but a relative may have admitted him and now you find him pitching a water softener. His plan will be to talk and talk, to tire you out, until you're ready to sign. Be impolite and ask right out:

"Hey buddy, why is it I can get the same thing at Sears for only three hundred?"

This will break up the rhythm of his discourse, and he may try to answer you. Whether he does, or whether he tries to brush the question aside and continue with his sales talk, ask the same question again after about two minutes.

You can throw in some extraneous and misleading comments, even if they're total lies, to break him up. It may be hard to get used to the idea of becoming a ruthless liar, but remember that a salesman is often exactly that. A comment such as:

"My aunt in Oshkosh bought one of those and it blew up the first day," will be a sure stopper. The salesman, if he's sharp, will reply:

"It can't be our brand. We don't sell them as far west as Oshkosh." You know that's a lie, so you throw in a bigger lie:

"Oh yes, it was your brand. It blew up, the fire department had to come, and my aunt sent me the newspaper clipping and it said right in the clipping, 'Your Brand' of water softener."

Get the idea? This sort of repartee can go on for awhile until one or both of you tires of it, and either he leaves voluntarily or at your insistence.

After the salesman leaves, you realize he never should have gotten in the door, and perhaps never should have arrived at your door. Irritated, you resolve that the next time....

The next day, the phone rings: "Hello, Mr. Smith, this is the Acme Donut Hole Company. We'd like to give you a free gift and demonstrate our new donut hole maker. What would be a good time?"

Think. Think hard.

"Come about seven." You know nobody'll be home then.

"Seven it is. See you at 301 West Street." That's just fine. You moved to East Street last month, but why tell them that? If you didn't move, tell them you did. It's always possible they won't take the hint, will call you back and ask where you live, but if you have a common name such as "Smith" you can run your finger down the page and pick out another one.

Turning to how to slip out of a deal if you feel it will turn sour, you can once more hide behind your "lawyer." Even if the deal is a straightforward one, such as buying a car, if the salesman asks you for a deposit, you can avoid writing him a check by telling him you have insufficient funds. He'll immediately come back with the suggestion you write a post-dated check, which is your cue to say:

"Oh, no, my lawyer told me never to write a post-dated check. He says I can be in double trouble if it bounces."

This doesn't have anything to do with anything, but it will stop a salesman cold. Your manner will help, too, if you just shake your head and repeat that your lawyer said "No" and that is that. No matter how hard he tries to pressure you, pretending you can't quite understand his explanations will frustrate him.

This is a good point to discuss an important aspect of the battle of wills between the salesman/con man and the client/victim. The motives may be honest or crooked, but the dynamics are the same. The salesman will use pressure, lies, and other deceptive tactics. Your defenses are more lies, temporizing, and a stubborn refusal. The salesman will perhaps even act boorish, try to make you look foolish, and embarrass you if you don't sign on the dotted line. If you cave in, you'll feel more foolish some days later. Use the time he's talking to think of an excuse not to sign. The lawyer story always works. Use it.

Safeguarding yourself against health frauds means more than just avoiding the snake-oil merchants/faith healers. Be careful with "real" doctors, too. Perhaps the best guide is the recommendation of a friend whose judgement you trust, when looking for a doctor.

Always get a second opinion whenever a doctor suggests either surgery or some radical treatment, such as radiation. If your life is on the line, a third opinion isn't too much. Placing yourself unhesitatingly in the hands of a knife-happy surgeon can be hazardous to your health.

Playing the market, unless you know a lot about it and do it for a hobby, can be hazardous to your wallet. If you get a tip on a stock, or an "investment," check it out with your lawyer, for real, before spending any money. If you're contacted by a boiler-room operation, use the same tactics as with other types of salespeople.

One exception is if a boiler room gets the wrong number. If they think you're Mister Jones, don't spoil the illusion. By all means order by phone, if they let you, and go along with anything they say.

If you're reasonably well off, and someone, working through a friend or an acquaintance, offers you a chance to get in on the ground floor of an investment in something new, take an extra step to protect yourself. Physically visit the premises, if they are within reach. If not, don't invest. You may get a nasty surprise, finding that a factory which is supposedly producing three hundred donut hole machines a day is shut up tightly.

Most passive and active defense is based on knowledge and common sense. The object is to protect yourself and your wallet from harm. Mostly, the means is to avoid getting "conned." It follows the old principle that an ounce of prevention is worth a pound of cure.

THE PRINCIPLES OF
COUNTER—ATTACK

As we've seen, sometimes passive and active defense are not enough, neither to protect us from being victimized nor to give us the satisfaction of retribution. There will be times when nothing less than a very aggressive measure will do.

Some people get very physical when they are angry. This is a release for emotion, but unfortunately it is also a felony to attack physically. If the attack is in front of witnesses, or if the other party chooses to prosecute, the fraud victim who lets himself be carried away by emotion will be in worse trouble than the con man because, as we've seen, fraud is hard to prosecute. In any event, the police will take a stand against anyone who takes the law into his own hands and beats up his exploiter. Their position is, under the law, that the proper response is to report the fraud to the authorities and let them handle it. A fraud does not constitute justification for a physical attack, under the law regarding self-defense, and the person who decides upon a physical attack has to face the prospect of criminal prosecution if he's seen and recognized.

An intelligent counter-attack consists of evaluating the situation and assigning priorities. The first step is to keep a low profile. In the sense of preparing a counter-attack, keeping a low profile means more than the defensive low profile. To keep the con artist off his guard, it's important that he not know that you, his victim, suspect anything. Setting him up while he thinks he's setting you up is simply good strategy.

The next principle is to gather the necessary information about the swindler, whom we'll call the "target" from now on. What information do you need? That depends on how you plan to strike back, and the amount of time and trouble you're willing to devote to the subject. At the least, you need the basic information to support your tactics. If, for example, you plan to strike back at him through the mail, all you need is his address for the basic methods.

With regards to gathering information in preparation for a counter-strike, it's important to consider the choice of target. Unfortunately, many swindlers are very slippery, and have left the scene before any of their victims become aware they've been had. If this happens to you, you'll feel very frustrated indeed, as your chances of counter-attack will have been foreclosed before you can start.

There is a possible solution to this problem. Any basic text in psychology explains the psychological mechanism known as "displacement," in which a person takes out his anger and frustration on another person or object, not the one who caused his anger. A person who's experienced a hard day at work because of the interpersonal conflict may come home and take it out on the family, for example. This "displacement" causes more problems in its wake, and is not a practical solution to such problems, when the object of the "displacement" *is an innocent person.*

If the target is another guilty one, the situation is totally different. In practical terms, if the con man who victimized you has already fled, you can attack another one. There is no shortage of fraud artists, and transferring your anger from one to another who's more available will do two things:

1. It will give you a psychologically healthy release for your anger and frustration.

2. By choosing another fraud artist, you'll be performing a useful public service. If you impede or break up his operation, you'll be saving other potential victims from going through the harrowing experience that you suffered.

This is one of the few instances in which a psychological defense mechanism, normally a compromise with reality, can offer the best solution to a problem, both in the inner world of feelings and in the outer world of reality. There is also a tactical advantage: By choosing another target, you have the option of being completely unknown to him, and therefore immune to any action he might want to take.

Another principle to follow is to plan carefully. Don't go off half-cocked, as hasty action, unless dictated by time pressure, is usually not the best. In some instances, it might be better to let your target go, and leave town unscathed, rather than carry out a premature attack that probably will not work very well. You can always select another swindler.

Finally, use the multiplier effect for maximum leverage. The multiplier effect means making others do the bulk of the work for you. You set off the spark, but the fire spreads on its own. In practical terms, it means causing your target more expense and trouble than you spent arranging it. We'll see how later.

COUNTER—ATTACKING
THROUGH THE MAILS

As many fraud operations use the mails, it's proper to use their own weapons against them. A good start is the postage-paid cards and envelopes. We've already seen in the section on active defense that sending them back will cause the target expense, but there is one step beyond that will multiply his expense.

Anyone with a business reply permit is obligated to pay this postage, no matter what. This means that, if you want to take a little time and trouble, you can wrap a brick in paper, attach a business reply card or envelope, mail it, and force him to pay whatever the cost is. If you want to be even nastier, fill a box with sand or dirt, seal it and attach the card, and think of the satisfaction in making him pay twenty or more dollars postage to receive a box of dirt.

Another way to use the mails against a fraud artist is to place an obviously fraudulent ad in his name in a publication. This will work only if he's going to be at the same mailing address long enough for the authorities to take notice. Here's how it works, in detail:

Your target is the "XYZ Company," which has run a successful scam for which they haven't been prosecuted because of a loophole in the law. Place an ad in a publication with the "XYZ" name and mailing address on it. You don't need to know their street address, if they're using a mail drop or a post office box. The authorities will find it in short order. The ad should read something like this:

"Guaranteed Cancer Cure — send ten dollars for information."

Or: "Become a member of the FBI — Diploma and badge guaranteed."

Many publications take the position that they'll print any ad as long as they get paid for it. It's usually possible to find one that will accept the ad. If you know the company's street address, you may be able to phone the ad in to the local newspaper, asking the newspaper to bill the company. It will usually cost less than ten dollars to place a classified ad.

If you've lodged a complaint against a swindler, but have seen no action because of a loophole, you can place an ad in his name to close the loophole. For example, if you answer an ad for a baldness cure, and the substance you get doesn't work, the police might tell you that the ad did not specifically guarantee that it would work for a particular individual, or some such nonsense. This indicates your line of approach. Place an ad, in the name of the company, that promises:

"Guaranteed to work on anyone."

Or: "Triple your money back guarantee."

This will not only close the loophole but give them a serious problem to boot. It may not even be necessary for you to pay for the ad. If the company's ad runs regularly in a certain publication, it's possible to phone the publication and claim to be a representative of the company, and order a change in the ad. You can instruct them to add the appropriate wording, and let them do the rest. This is a perfect example of the multiplier effect.

In plain language, what you've just done is to "frame" your target. By a sophisticated means, you've planted evidence that will facilitate prosecution and cause additional problems with his running the scam. If you want to get really serious about framing him, you can use the mail for it.

With the furor over "controlled substances" in this country, you can send him drugs in the mail. An envelope with a baggie of cocaine, if you have access to illegal drugs, will serve the purpose. An incriminating note, written on a rental typewriter, can accompany the cocaine, to nail the door shut. The note might say:

"Here's the stuff you wanted. Please hurry up and pay me. You still owe me for the last time."

Of course, leave the note unsigned.

There is no assurance that this will result in the con man's going to prison. However, although an unsigned note and an envelope of drugs, found by the police after you tip them off in an anonymous call, may not result in an air-tight case, it will still be an annoyance, and the con man will have a hard time explaining how the material got into his mail. In the same way, if he tries to claim he did not order the change in the wording of his ad, nobody will believe him, and the odds of a conviction will have suddenly improved.

The ultimate weapon you can use against the swindler who operates his scheme through the mail is to file a false change of address card for him (or against him, if you prefer) with the Post Office. Select an address in another city to cause further confusion. If you want to get his mail utterly lost, divert it to a mail drop in another city, leaving instructions that they are to forward the mail to an address you select. This address will be false, of course.

Diverting his mail may not work for long before he checks it out with the Post Office and discovers the false address change. He'll annul it, of course, but it will still mean he'll have lost a quantity of checks addressed to him

The most important aspect of counter-attacking through the mail is not to get crossed up and use methods that wipe each other out. Sending him heavy business reply mail will be a wasted effort if you use a change of address card on him.

PUTTING THE HEAT
ON THE BOILER ROOM

Boiler room operations, using banks of telephones, are most vulnerable at one point — the phones. Put out the phones and they're dead in the water. There are a number of ways of attacking their phones, but first you need to know where they are and what numbers.

Many boiler room salespeople do not normally give you their phone numbers, instead arranging an appointment for one of their sales reps to visit you, or gaining your agreement to buy stock or precious metals options, etc. Therefore, if you get a phone call of the boiler room type, the first priority is to find out the phone number from which the party is calling. A simple way is:

"Hey, that sounds great, but there's somebody at the door. Can I call you right back in a couple of minutes? What's the number there?"

There are only two possible responses. One is agreement, and disclosing the number. The other is to tell you that he or she will call you back in a few minutes.

If you get the second response, all is not lost. When the boiler room operator calls back, listen to the pitch, and write down any pertinent information. If there's a street address given, it may be possible to go there and, using the stalled car trick, obtain the phone number. This might be necessary because fly-by-night operators are not at an address long enough to be listed in a telephone directory.

If you're being invited to a sales office for a "demonstration" or other purpose, by all means go. Stay just long enough to note the phone number or numbers, keeping in mind that there is usually more than one.

A problem may arise if the phone call is from an out of town boiler room with WATS lines. WATS stands for Wide Area Telephone Service, and is a bulk rate offered by the phone company for heavy long-distance users. If the call is from out of town, you may not be able to track down the address and phone number as easily. However, many public libraries stock out of town directories, which will make your task easier.

Once you've obtained the obnoxious number, the next step is to decide your course of action. Plan carefully, keeping in mind one action may cancel out the effect of another.

The first, and obvious step, is to interrupt their phone service. The directory will give you the business office number for each phone exchange. A call to the business office, representing yourself as the office manager of the "XYZ Company," and telling the service rep the office is closing for a week, will result in the lines being disconnected at your request. It's that simple.

While you're at it, you might call the power company to have the electricity cut off on the same date. Not having a phone readily available to call and find out why the power's off will delay them further.

It's expecting too much to think this will interrupt their operations for more than a day. It's also a trick that you can use only once. To continue the disruption of their "business," you need other means.

Keeping their lines tied up is another way to slow them down. Placing an ad offering a house or car for sale at an irresistible price will keep the phone calls coming in for awhile.

One method that worked and kept a business's lines tied up for three days was a classified ad offering "free green stamps" to the first thousand people who called a certain number.

Note that in all of these methods there was no need for you to call the boiler room yourself with any disruptive calls. The multiplier effect assured that one phone call from you resulted in hours of hassle for them.

Another way to tie up the phone lines is to offer a free keg of a new brand of beer, delivered to the home, to the first thousand people who call a certain number. For some of the more outlandish ideas, the classified advertising department of a newspaper may be reluctant to accept them.

The way around this is to have a quick printer run some flyers for you. As we've seen previously, printers don't question closely

170

material run for a paying customer, as long as it's not blatantly illegal, libelous, or pornographic. An 8 1/2 x 11" flyer on cheap white paper, printed on one side only, will run you about five dollars a hundred, and quantity price breaks are available.

Two possible wordings for such flyers are as follows:

FREE INTRODUCTORY OFFER!

NEW BEER DISTRIBUTOR MAKING YOU "AN OFFER YOU CAN'T REFUSE." WE'LL GIVE YOU A KEG OF THE BRAND OF BEER OF YOUR CHOICE ABSOLUTELY FREE, JUST TO GET ACQUAINTED!

NOTHING ELSE TO BUY! NO CONTRACTS TO SIGN! NO OBLIGATION OF ANY SORT!

WE'LL DELIVER ANYTIME DAY OR NIGHT, AT YOUR CONVENIENCE. HOLD A NEIGHBORHOOD BEER BUST, AND TELL YOUR FRIENDS!

WE'LL SUPPLY THE KEG, TAPPER, TUB, ICE, AND PLASTIC GLASSES FOR ONE HUNDRED GUESTS.

NOW HERE'S THE CATCH: WE'LL ALSO GIVE YOU A COPY OF OUR PRICE LIST. REMEMBER, THE FIRST KEG IS ABSOLUTELY FREE, BUT WHEN YOU DECIDE TO HAVE ANOTHER PARTY, YOU'LL REMEMBER THE PRICES WE CHARGE AND YOU'LL CALL US FOR SURE!

FOR YOUR FREE INTRODUCTORY KEG OF BEER, CALL: 123-4567

— — — — — — — — — — — — —

BOTTLE CAP COLLECTOR NEEDS BOTTLE CAPS

COLLECTOR WILL PAY FOR BOTTLE CAPS. PRICES RANGE FROM ONE DOLLAR EACH FOR COMMON ONES UP TO TWENTY DOLLARS FOR HARD TO FIND BOTTLE CAPS.

CALL 123-4567 TO FIND OUT WHAT YOUR BOTTLE CAPS ARE WORTH.

It won't be necessary for you to spend hours in parking lots placing them on windshields. Leave a short stack of them in every store in a shopping complex, and enough people will pick them up to make the effort worthwhile.

CRAMPING HIS STYLE

This category involves carrying out or provoking actions that will physically interfere with your target's operations. Not all fraud artists are vulnerable to this, but those who are will suffer.

This simple action you can take will work only if the target has a fenced-in yard or parking lot. A water-softener peddler usually needs a parking lot for the trucks used for installation. If the gate is closed by a chain and padlock, putting an extra padlock on the chain one dark night will cause some consternation the next morning. A good padlock will cost upwards of five dollars, which might seem too much money for just a few hours' inconvenience. A tube of cyanoacrylate glue (Krazy Glue) squirted into the lock will seal it shut, making it unnecessary for you to buy another lock to block access.

If you have the target's address, as you need to for the lock trick, there are other choices open to you. One is to place a classified ad that will bring people to his office by the scores or by the hundreds. Free green stamps is one possibility.

Another gimmick that will bring people flocking to his door is to have a quick printer turn out coupons worded as follows:

LUCKY FINDER PROGRAM

THE PERSON WHO FINDS THIS COUPON WILL RECIEVE TEN DOLLARS UPON BRINGING IT TO 123 WEST 45TH STREET. PRESENT THIS COUPON AND GET YOUR TEN DOLLARS.

NOTHING TO SIGN!

NOTHING TO BUY!

Coupons holding that wording will fit three to a page, with room left over for the company name and address at the bottom. When ordering such printing, do not include the company's phone number if the object is to bring people to the office. Some might phone to confirm the offer is still running.

Another flyer to attract crowds can read like this:

ATTENTION RECYCLERS!

THE ABC COMPANY IS JOINING THE COMMUNITY IN AN EFFORT TO CLEAN UP THE ENVIRONMENT BY RECYCLING CANS, BOTTLES, AND MORE! BRING YOUR RECYCLABLES TO THE ADDRESS AT THE BOTTOM AND RECEIVE CASH FOR THEM!

PRICES ARE AS FOLLOWS:

CANS	$1.00 each
BOTTLES	$1.50 each
TIRES	$5.00 each
NEWSPAPERS	$1.00/pound

FOR PROMPT PAYMENT, DELIVER MATERIAL BETWEEN NINE AND FIVE WEEKDAYS. IF DELIVERED AT OTHER TIMES, LEAVE THE ARTICLES IN THE YARD, FILL OUT THE COUPON AT THE BOTTOM OF THIS PAGE WITH YOUR NAME, ADDRESS, AND THE AMOUNT YOU BROUGHT, AND WE'LL SEND YOU A CHECK THE NEXT MORNING!

NAME
ADDRESS
NUMBER OF CANS:
NUMBER OF BOTTLES:
NUMBER OF TIRES:
NEWSPAPERS, POUNDS   TOTAL AMOUNT $

Something that will work well against an unethical used-car dealer is a flier advertising a beer bust:

COME ONE, COME ALL!

TENTH ANNIVERSARY BEER BUST AT MODEL MOTORS,

123 WEST FOURTH STREET.

MIDDLEVILLE, USA.

STARTS AT TEN A.M. AND CONTINUES UNTIL DARK!

ALL THE BEER YOU CAN DRINK! FREE BUFFET-STYLE FOOD!

STEAK AND RIBS ON THE GRILL! CORN COBS AND COWBOY BEANS!

COME AND CELEBRATE WITH US! EACH PERSON ATTENDING WILL QUALIFY FOR THE DRAWING FOR A NEW CADILLAC LIMO BEING GIVEN AWAY IN CELEBRATION OF OUR TENTH ANNIVERSARY!

NOTHING TO BUY! NOTHING TO SIGN!

DOOR PRIZES OF FREE COLOR TVS GIVEN AWAY EVERY HOUR!

BE THERE!

This has to work with a flyer, rather than an advertisement, because no newspaper is likely to accept anything as outlandish as that, but a quick printer will.

It helps to tailor the flyer to the sort of target you're attacking. A water-softener pusher would more logically be giving away water softeners, not Cadillacs. A pyramid sales office would give away almost anything, but the door prizes would be cases of their merchandise. Plan carefully, and the effect will be devastating!

Two "quickies" that will add to the swindler's troubles start with classified ads you place in his name in the local paper. One reads like this:

FREE HOROSCOPE
Your future foretold.
No fee, no obligation.
Call 123-4567
HOROSCOPES UNLIMITED

The other one reads:

HIGH-PAYING JOBS, NO EXPERIENCE NEEDED
234-5678
ABC EMPLOYMENT

Both of these will result in phone calls. Note the company names are different. There's a reason for this. When you call in the ads, it might seem suspicious if the same company offered both horoscopes and jobs. The mailing address is the same, but the name is different.

A variation is to give the address in the ad. Employment ads are more likely to bring in walk-in traffic, making them the better choice.

INSIDE WORK

In some instances, you'll have access to the fraud artist's premises. The scam might be a pyramid sales scheme, or other type which makes use of an "office" or "warehouse." As one of the "customers," you may be able to walk in and stay, at least long enough to counter-attack effectively.

It might seem superficially attractive to have "the run of the place," but it isn't necessarily true. Part of your purpose is to strike without detection, and becoming too well known may expose your suspicion. It's best to blend in with the crowd, and do your work casually, without attracting unusual attention.

Exactly what you can do depends on how much access you have to the premises. Some measures you can take require very little, only getting in the front door. We'll consider these first:

If the "business" has a waiting room, lobby, or other area open to the public, and if there are seats and tables with magazines, you can invest a few dollars and cause the fraud artist some embarrassment. Buy some pornographic magazines. They need not be new. Some second-hand, well-thumbed ones will serve the purpose. The sicker they seem, the better. Don't waste your money on those of the *Playboy* and *Penthouse* genre. Buy the ones devoted to sadomasochistic practices, with photos of nude women in chains and the like. Homosexual and lesbian material is equally good. Type up labels with the company name on them, and affix them to the magazines. If you know the name of a specific person, use that. Then go about planting them.

Even if you're a total stranger, gaining access to the lobby is usually easy to accomplish without arousing suspicion. Walk in, with several magazines in your hand, and sit down. Place them on the table, pick up another one, and start to read. The receptionist will notice you soon, at which point you ask for a non-existent person. The discussion ends with your admitting you got the wrong address, and you leave.

If you know someone at the "office," simply bring the doctored magazines with you when you come for an appointment and drop them off at a convenient moment in an appropriate spot.

If you're a total stranger, and have no business there, you still may be able to gain limited access by asking to use the rest room. This will usually cause no difficulty at all if you're well-dressed, well-spoken, and look "respectable." Carrying an attache case will help, in more ways than one.

The attache case contains several plastic bags full of quick-setting cement or plaster, which you pour into the toilet and sink drains. Once the cement sets, it will require a plumber to remove. For best results, the premises should be small, for if there's more than one toilet, the inconvience will not be as great. Of course, if you can manage to block every sink and toilet in the place, so much the better.

If you have more than just casual access to the premises, there are other choices open to you. One simple one is to smuggle in a gallon can of gasoline, if the local fire regulations have strict prohibitions regarding storage of gasoline indoors. Once you "plant" the can, in a broom closet or storage area, a discreet phone call to the fire marshall's office will start the ball rolling.

The story you tell the fire marshall might go like this:

"I work at the XYZ Company, but I don't want to give my name. The boss keeps a gallon of gasoline next to the furnace, and I'm afraid it might blow up one of these days. I told him I didn't think it was a good idea, but he told me to shut up and mind my own business. Can you do anything about this? I'm afraid of losing my job."

Another counter-measure you can take, depending on exactly how much access you have to the premises, is to stink them out. The first step is to buy chicken parts at the supermarket. They should be uncooked, and frozen. If they come from the fresh market case, pop them into your freezer for a couple of days, to freeze them solid. Keep the parts individually wrapped in waxed paper.

Chicken, when spoiled, has one of the most offensive odors of all meat. Hiding pieces of chicken in an office or shop will make the place unliveable when the meat starts to putrify. That's why it's a good idea to start with frozen pieces of fresh meat, as there will

178

be no odor when you smuggle the meat into the place. You'll have a comfortable time cushion to plant it and get away.

Planting it where it won't be easily found is the next problem. Although placing it in the air conditioning and heating ducts is an ideal method, it's not likely that you'll be able to unscrew the registers unobserved. Some good places are:

Behind or underneath the seat cushions on a couch.

In the top folds of the drapes.

Open a drawer all the way, and throw the meat behind it.

Behind or underneath heavy pieces of furniture.

Inside boxes containing other items, such as envelopes.

Behind books on shelves.

Under the carpet in a dark corner, if you can pry it up unobserved.

In the walls, if you can unscrew light switch plates unobserved.

On the topmost shelves in closets.

If there's a clothes closet, inside the pockets. This will work especially well if people leave clothing there for several days. Even if they take their coats and jackets home each night, they don't all check the pockets each time, and might take some of these smelly time-bombs home with them.

Of course, unwrap the meat before placing it. You don't want the waxed paper to protect the furniture from the juices of decomposition.

Another means of sabotage, in which they'll do the dirty work for you, is the fake furniture polish can. Removing the label from a can of furniture polish and putting it on a can of spray paint or stain remover will destroy the finish when sprayed on a piece of furniture. If finding furniture polish with a removable label is impossible, have your own printed.

You'll find, with a little imagination, there are many possibilities for retaliation against a swindler if you have access to where he lives or works. The risks are small, the effects great.

DIRECT ACTION

Direct action methods are quick, and easy to use. Sometimes they're all you can use. If the swindler does not have an office or warehouse, if he's the type who operates out of his briefcase and has no permanent address, but is staying in a hotel or motel, your choice of targets is limited. A few quick and dirty methods may be all you can use in the limited time before he leaves town.

Almost everyone has a car these days, and that's a logical starting point. The car may belong to the swindler, or it may be a rental, but working on the car will at least deny him the use of his wheels. If he owns it, so much the better.

A rule of thumb is, if it's a current model car, it may be a rental. A car more than two years old is not likely to be a rental car. Some rental agencies use window stickers, distinctive license plate frames, or other means to identify their cars.

One of the simplest means of denying him the use of the car, and probably causing him some repair bills, is to squirt cyanoacrylate glue in his locks. This glue sets in a minute or less, and is very hard to remove. If he normally leaves his car unlocked, a squirt in the ignition lock will prevent him from starting the car. If you have enough time, and enough glue, squirting a film of glue on all his door gaskets will keep him out of his car.

Cyanoacrylate glue is commonly available under various trade names, such as "Krazy Glue." It will glue almost anything to almost anything else. A few other uses to which you can put this glue is to squirt some into the door and window locks of his hotel or motel room. The moments when he's trying to get into his car will give you an opportunity to do this. If he has a permanent address, you can do the locks there.

A very quick and dirty method of attacking his car is to run a point of a can opener down the entire side of his car. A scratch such as this, running through several body panels, is expensive to repair, and is worth doing if it's his personal car. If it's a rental, it won't hold him up for a minute.

His car finish is also vulnerable to spray paint or paint thinner. Either one will ruin his paint job. He won't care if it's a rental car, but in that case, spray the paint on his windows.

Occasionally, it's possible to find some zany bumper stickers, with legends that can cause embarrassment or more serious trouble for the driver of a car that has such a sticker displayed. Slogans such as:

"Follow me if you're gay"

"God is dead"

might cause a serious incident for the driver. More inflammatory slogans, especially those with a racial content, will almost guarantee that sooner or later he'll be rammed "accidentally on purpose" or become involved in an incident.

Some printers specialize in printing bumper stickers in quantities of one or two. They may cost as much as two dollars each, but that's not much at today's prices.

IMPERSONATION

Impersonating the swindler is a very effective technique, especially as you won't have to do it in person. A vast amount of business today is done by telephone, which makes it relatively easy to play this game. Swindlers do it all the time.

With even a little imagination and time, you can do an incredible amount of damage by pretending to be the swindler. Starting with some of the simplest methods, you can work up to some more sophisticated and far-reaching ones.

What you can do by phone, as with everything else, depends on your target's situation and how much you know about him. Not every method will apply to everyone.

If your con man, for example, is staying in a hotel room, as in **running phoney job interviews, you can call room service in his** name and have unwanted meals sent up. You can call the desk to have the hotel rent a car in his name. If he already has a rented car, you can have it sent back, if the hotel has a parking garage in which the client turns over the key to the attendant.

Using the telephone is vital in the "crossfire" technique. This is when you set one person against another, slipping away when the fight starts. Here's how it works:

You call the hotel garage, impersonating the con man, and order the car washed. The reply may be that the hotel does not offer the service, or there will be a slight delay. Find out the name of the person who answers and then call the hotel office to complain about this. Be utterly unreasonable, and use obscene language, especially if the person who answers the phone is female. The point is to be as abusive as possible, which will result in the clerk putting the manager on the line. At this point, you say:

"If I wanted to talk to you, you #$$%&*, I'd have asked for you," and hang up.

Immediately call the swindler. Identify yourself as Joe Blow, the garage attendant, and tell him what you think of him, and add if you ever see him, you'll get violent. During this call, be as abusive as possible also.

If the swindler operates out of an office building, or other rented premises, calling the landlord or manager and becoming abusive will start the ball rolling. The chances of success are much greater in this instance, because the swindler's "company" will most likely have several employees. In the case of the hotel manager, he might realize, if the swindler's voice is quite different from yours, that all is not as it seems, but when there are several people on the premises, and if you just identify yourself as "Acme Vacuum Cleaners," the crossfire technique is likely to work.

Impersonating the swindler, or one of his employees, is useful in another way in a "boiler room" operation. You can call potential victims yourself, making the most outrageously fraudulent claims on the phone. If you choose to do this, select your list carefully. Calling attorneys, prosecutors, postal inspectors and police officers, if you have their home numbers, will improve the chances of getting results. So will calling officers of the Chamber of Commerce and Better Business Bureau. The chances of getting their home numbers are much greater, as typically police officers, judges, prosecutors, and the like have unlisted numbers.

If there's a consumer protection group in the area, they will be a very good choice. Tracking down and stimulating official action against consumer ripoffs is their specialty, and they're the ones likely to make the most intense efforts.

You can also use impersonation as a follow-up to having the utilities cut off. After the con man makes the necessary calls to have the electricity and phone service restored, you can call up the business offices of the telephone and utility companies and berate **them for being so stupid as to accept a phoney call. Again, the key is to be extremely abusive. This will work best with the phone** company, because there is an FCC regulation regarding obscene language used on the telephone. Normally, the telephone company is very lackadaisical in its attention to this, as anyone who has tried to complain about obscene phone calls knows, but when someone does it to them, they will move. The retaliation will be, if they take it seriously enough, to cut off the phone service permanently.

This technique can be so effective that it's worth laying out in detail:

"Business office, Mary speaking."

"Hello, I'm calling about that stupid business where you cut off my lines yesterday. How could you be so stupid?"

"I'm sorry, sir, but someone called here, claiming to be from your company, and said you were closing the office for a week. We had no way of knowing it wasn't legitimate."

"What the #$%%& is the matter with you people? After the high rates that you #$%&%&s charge me, you can't even keep your heads on straight?" (Note the unreasonable tone, and the ignoring of the business representative's explanation.)

"Sir, you don't need to use language like that. I'm only trying to help you."

"Help me? You can help me by #$%%&%%$$*** my **&%$#$%. You and your company can't even #$%&*** help yourselves."

"If you continue to use language like that, I'll have to report you to my supervisor."

"Go ahead. She's probably a #$$%***& like you, too. In fact, when I get back to the office, I'll probably call the president of your #$%&*** company and tell him that, too." (Note the subtle touch here. Telephone company offices with electronic switching equipment have the facilities to determine from what phone a call originates. You take care of the question of why he isn't calling from the number in question very effectively with that last sentence.)

"This is the supervisor. What do you mean, using language like that to Mary?"

"She's heard it before, just like you have, you #$%&**. You sound just as #$%**&%$ stupid as she does. Are you going to give me the same bullshit excuses she did?"

"I don't know what Mary told you, but your using language like that won't help."

"I don't care what you tell me. Both of you are #$%*** stupid and I don't see how you keep your #$$%** jobs. If you two #$%** worked for me, you'd be out on the #$%**& street."

"If you don't stop using that abusive language, I'm going to hang up, and disconnect your service."

"You don't dare, you $%&#*." (Sooner or later, the supervisor will hang up on you. That is when you go into phase two. You call up the manager of the office of the President, and become as abusive to the secretary who answers as you were to the business office people.)

"Those #$%$#* idiots at the business office were really nasty and stupid, those #$%*&%$. The dumb #$%*&% threatened to cut off my phone, the #$%&%&*."

With a few such phone calls, made from a pay phone, you can cause your target such grief that the effort for you will be well worthwhile.

PLANTED EVIDENCE

If you're really serious about hitting back hard at the swindler, you might consider framing him on a drug charge. Doing it by mail is uncertain, but physically planting the evidence will work every time.

Planting evidence is sometimes known as "flaking," a term that refers to the evidence falling on him as a snowflake would. You have several choices available, if you decide to flake him. If you have access at all to his hotel room, office, or other premises, planting an envelope of drugs is easy. It takes only a moment to open a desk drawer and drop it in. Asking to use the toilet gives you the chance to slip it in the medicine chest.

Much depends on your having access to "hard" drugs, and the amount of money you want to spend. The law in some states distinguishes between "users" and "pushers," with the distinction depending on the quantity found. It's worth checking this out before starting.

In some instances, it will be easier to plant it in his car than anywhere else. One bonus of this is that some states have laws stating the car is to be confiscated if drugs are found inside it. Whether the car is a rental or his personal one, this will make waves, as even if it's a rental car, the rental company will sue him for the value of the car, adding to his problems.

Informing the police is the touchy part. The police receive crank calls each day. They also receive spurious "leads" from malicious people. To make the police act, you have to be convincing. At the start, you're handicapped because under no circumstances do you wish to identify yourself.

The first step is to call police headquarters and ask for the narcotics detectives. When one gets on the line, one story that you might use is the following:

"There's a new man in town. He's trying to cut into the action. His car is parked in front of ——— and he has an envelope of smack in his glove compartment."

If the car is locked, you might have to slip it in through a crack in the window, to land on the seat. Another possibility is to put it inside the hubcap, which is one possible hiding place for someone carrying contraband.

The detective might want to know who you are or why you're telling him. Naturally, you won't give your name. You also should be aware that the detective will wonder which of the regular dealers is informing, if he accepts your hypothesis. If he does not recognize the voice, he may not accept your story, which is why you should whisper into the phone to leave this doubt open. He won't be able to say you are one of the regulars, but neither will he be able to say you're not.

It is a psychological quirk that people are more ready to believe a story someone tells against himself. You can take advantage of this by using a story against yourself if the opportunity comes. A couple of possibilities are:

You're a drug addict, and the target sold you impure stuff.

If the detective insists on knowing your motivation, you can tell him outright you're a jealous lover (it's all right to admit being **homosexual for the story — the detective doesn't know who you are) who is informing just to get his betrayer in trouble.**

If you use a convincing manner, and a have little luck, the police will get a search warrant and follow up on your call. This points up one advantage of planting the evidence in a car. The police can, if the car is unlocked or if the stash is in a hubcap, make a discreet search without the bother of a warrant. When they find it, they go back and get a warrant to make it legal.

You can use almost anything as planted evidence. In a state or city which has strict gun laws, planting a firearm will result in an arrest. Stolen property is another good one. Whatever you choose, you must tailor it to the local conditions, and be prepared to improvise.

LONG-RANGE TECHNIQUES

Often, the fraud artist is unapproachable by direct means. He may be literally a fly-by-night, here just long enough to work his scam and gone the next day. If he's using an alias, for all practical purposes he's gone. The police may be able to trace him, but a private citizen may have a much harder time of it. While there are skip-tracing techniques, they cost time and money. Not all of them are as simple as sending an envelope to the target through the mail with a "Return Receipt Requested, Show Address Where Delivered."

The reason for this is the swindler is a pro at doing a disappearing act. Typically, he'll make a hasty exit, leaving no forwarding address. Without time, effort, and the resources of an organization, the victim has little chance of finding him.

There are a few ways in which the victim can try to find his victimizer, without excessive time, cost, and effort. The key is that the swindler conforms to a pattern. He tends to use a successful method again and again.

An example would be a fraud artist who advertises a "vacation" contest in a national magazine.[1] He'll run the ad, wait for a very few weeks to get the responses, mail out the "winning" letters, collect his money, and he'll be gone. If he's used a post office box, one day the box will just continue to fill up, as he'll stop coming to collect the mail. If he uses a letter drop, he'll rent it for only two months, leaving no forwarding address when his rental expires. Tracing him down to the letter drop will usually be futile, as the people who operate letter drops understand they're not to inquire too closely of their clients, and they don't seek information the client may feel is his business alone. They are professionally unhelpful to any seeking information about their clients. As often the fraud artist will pay in cash, there'll be no record of payment that is traceable.

The alert victim can, with a little luck, sometimes discover where the swindler has moved. He may, for example, notice another similar "vacation" ad a few months later in another national magazine. Of course, the address will be different, as will the "company" name, and the vacation spot and accompanying photographs may not be the same, but the overall scheme will be remarkably similar.

One outstanding similarity may be the wording of the ad. People do have characteristic ways of expressing themselves, and often a distinctive pattern of expression will surface. The victim who feels he's read the ad before may well have. The ad may contain the word "hurry" several times, or the phrase "limited time only."

There's reason for caution, however. Keep in mind that swindlers, who have no qualms about victimizing people through unethical, illegal, and deceptive practices, are not above plagiarism, and one swindler may copy the text of another's ad remorselessly.

Another reason for a fraud artist's being out of reach is those who operate by mail are often in another city, and often this is not an accident, as they want to be out of reach. In fact, they may not even run their rackets in the same state in which they have their headquarters, in order to make a casual investigation difficult for most of their victims. A swindler who is running an investment racket will not welcome casual visitors arriving at the site of his "plant" or "mine" and inspecting the facilities. Out-of-state land swindlers don't want their clients to know the parcels they're buying are under water or on top of a mountain.

Sometimes, the swindle is very modest, and on the borderline of legality, and the fraud artist may stay in place for years, secure in the knowledge the victims are not going to look him up for the small amount of money involved. Examples are the various distributors of vitamins, diet pills, and popular music recordings that advertise on television. Typically, the commercial will ask the viewer to send his check or money order to a local P.O. box, which may well be in Portland or Phoenix, while the home office is in Boston. The customer who feels the quality of the records or tapes are not worth the money, or who feels he or she has been ripped off in the purchase of the pills, will usually take the point of view that it's not worth the hassle for "only" twenty dollars. The psychologically compelling thing is that twenty dollars seems to be the magic figure right now (late 1984). Just as it is a small enough amount for most people to risk on a purchase sight-unseen, so it is not a large enough amount for most people to disturb themselves in trying for a refund or reporting the transaction to the authorities.

A special block of techniques will enable you, the victim, to reach these remote fraud artists. Most of them are adaptations of more conventional techniques. In one sense, the long-range methods are easier and safer to use than most of the conventional ones, as they work at several thousand miles distance, in some cases.

The simplest, least costly, and safest technique is to re-route the mail through change-of-address cards. That's right, cards, plural, because often the swindlers operate through a P.O. box in your city but have their headquarters elsewhere. You'll see the main address on the package you receive, if you send for their material.

Hitting the local P.O. box first will produce the most results fastest, because that's where the checks are coming in. Mailing a change of address card to the "Postmaster" of the ZIP code at which the box is located will do it. When you do this, you can make an extra preparation, if you want to spend the time and money. Divert the mail to a local mail drop[2] which you'll have rented for the minimum period, and instruct the operator of the mail drop to send what he receives on to another address. This is a good way to "lose" the mail permanently.

Mailing a change of address card to the postmaster in the city where the "company" has its headquarters will divert the mail from the head office. This might have even more serious effects if the local operator simply sends the mail from his P.O. box to the main office. If, on the other hand, he opens up a local bank account for the deposit of the income from the local P.O. box, he may have another means of transferring the money home.

Long-range retaliation works best if you're willing to spend a small amount of money to have some material printed by a local quick printer. Here is a list of the basics. Pick the ones that suit your situation:

1. Letterhead for the swindler's "company."
2. Letterhead for a fictitious company, totally unrelated to the swindler's outfit.
3. Invoices for the swindler's company.
4. Tickets to a non-existent concert or sporting event.
5. Mailing labels.
6. Envelopes to match the "letterheads."

Each of these has its uses. First, the letterhead for the swindler's company is useful in generating fake mail from him, which can lead him into an indictment, or at least complications with the other companies with which he does business. For example, a letter to the local television station that runs his commercials can cause him complications, if it orders the series of commercials extended beyond the original contract, or cancelled, or shifted to three o'clock in the morning. Another way in which you can cause him problems by a spurious letter to the TV station is to order a change of wording displayed on the screen. A simple change of address will have the same effect as a change of address at the post office.

What do you do if you don't know what his letterhead is like? That's really no problem. Either write the "company" a letter on an innocuous subject to provoke a reply and copy from the letterhead they send you, or make up your own. Businesses often change the design of their letterheads, and anyone doing business with your target will probably not suspect forgery if he gets a totally new letterhead.

Another use for the letterhead is to generate spurious and indictable frauds on behalf of the target. One good possibility is to write a letter, offering tickets to a non-existent concert or other event, enclosing a pair of tickets in each letter, and addressing the envelopes to people chosen at random from a city directory or phone book. It need not be a fancy job, as a plain boilerplate text will do. It might run like this:

ONE TIME OFFER

For the first and only time in this city, ABC Marketing Corporation is offering discount tickets to the forthcoming concert by the famous rock group, FIVE CAR CRASH. These tickets, for the May 20 performance at the Colossus Theatre, normally sell for twenty dollars each. With this special offer, you can buy a pair of them for only ten dollars each. Send your check to:

> ABC Marketing Corp.
> Post Office Box 123
> Localville, USA 12345

It might seem odd to include the tickets with the letter, but for your purpose it will work very well, as the tickets really have no value, being forgeries, and there are some who will send in checks to the "ABC Marketing Corp." The fun will begin when the ticket-holders, especially the ones who sent in their checks, arrive at the "concert" and find it was never scheduled.

Fake invoices, a common scam, will help to make things hot at long-range for your target. To ensure a prosecution, you must make certain these invoices do not go through the normal channels of the companies that receive them. Normally, a swindler will send invoices to various companies for non-existent products or services[3] in the hope that some of them will go through the accounting department routinely and be paid without being questioned. That's not quite what you want.

You can select a list of companies from any list — the phone book, the *Thomas Register*, etc. Make out an invoice for each one. Also type a covering letter, such as this one:

Dear Sirs;

This is a duplicate of the invoice we sent you three months ago, and which your company has not seen fit to pay. It is incredible that a company such as yours should be staffed by such incompetent and immoral people.

If this invoice is not paid within ten days, we will take other steps.

> Yours truly,

Enclose an invoice dated three months earlier. This will rattle cages and get attention. Inevitably, one or more of the companies involved will report the incidents to the postal authorities.

Another long-range retaliation technique which can have the most far-reaching consequences of all is the "free sample." Using the letterhead of a spurious company, you send the target some free samples of various items. One such is a variation of the furniture polish technique. Removing the label from a can of spray paint, you replace it with a simple printed label that says "PRODUCT 3955," and ship it to your target with a covering letter from the company that allegedly produces the item. The letter might read like this:

FABULOUS FURNITURE FINISHES
West 45th Street
Newtown, USA

Mr. Edgar Odious,
Sales Manager
Sleazy Marketing, Inc.

Dear Mr. Odious;

The enclosed sample of furniture polish is a new kind developed by our research department, and which is not yet in the test-marketing stage. We're sending samples of it at random to companies and individuals all over the country to determine user response.

Please accept this sample can with my compliments. Use it on your furniture as you would any other product. You'll find it works best if you spray the whole piece of furniture at once and let the polish stand for at least two minutes before buffing it to a high polish with a clean, soft rag.

I hope you like it, and that you'll let me know of your experience with it. If at any time you'd like more samples, please do not hesitate to ask.

Yours truly,

James Niceguy
Sales Manager

The list of products you can substitute, contaminate, or otherwise alter is almost endless. You can add hair remover to shampoo or hair dressing. Adding a fabric dye to a detergent or fabric softener will affect a whole washerload of clothing. Adding an abrasive to lubricating oil will cause accelerated wear to any machinery to which it's applied. Automobile engine oil is a good example, and so is chassis grease.

Truly, no swindler is out of your reach. If you can find him, you can cause him endless aggravation with the techniques described here, and with others limited only by your imagination.

NOTES

1. See the chapter on postal frauds.

2. *Directory of Mail Drops,* current edition, Loompanics Unlimited, PO Box 1197, Port Townsend, WA 98368.

3. See chapter on business frauds.

YOU WILL ALSO WANT TO READ: